YOUR FUTURE IN BANKING

YOUR FUTURE IN BANKING

Ralph E. Boynton

RICHARDS ROSEN PRESS, INC.,
New York, New York 10010

Standard Book Number: 08239-0360-5
Library of Congress Catalog Number: 76-445

Published in 1965, 1976 by Richards Rosen Press, Inc.
29 East 21st Street, New York City, N.Y. 10010

Manufactured in the United States of America

Second Edition

About the Author

Ralph E. Boynton, son of a New England banker, was employed for more than thirty years by Bank of America. He retired at age 56 as a vice president to devote full time to his interest in manpower problems. Recently he became president of a firm involved in manpower research, development and training. Mr. Boynton was born in Massachusetts and raised in southern California. He is a graduate of Occidental College, Los Angeles where he was elected to Phi Beta Kappa. In addition to specialized studies in personnel administration at the California Institute of Technology, Pasadena he completed the Stonier Graduate School of Banking program at Rutgers University in New Brunswick, New Jersey.

After joining Bank of America's main office in Hollywood as a messenger in 1937 Mr. Boynton progressed to bookkeeper, teller, and note clerk, then entered the operations and personnel field as an assistant operations officer. He was promoted to staff training officer in the educational department in 1942. In 1946, after four years of service as an officer in the U.S. Marine Corps, he was named assistant to the district operations officer for a major downtown Los Angeles branch and then advanced to assistant director of staff training in charge of the bank's southern division in 1950 and was promoted from this position to director of training in 1955 and vice president in 1961. He then was given responsibility for training and development system wide and for a number of related personnel functions including college and executive recruiting.

Mr. Boynton devoted several years to the Training Committee of the American Bankers Association and to the Education Committee of the Credit Research Foundation, National Association of Credit Management. During nearly a decade he served the federal government, first as a member of the U.S. Secretary of Labor's Committee on Specialized Personnel, then as a member of the National Manpower Advisory Committee to the United States Secretaries of Labor and Health Education and Welfare and finally as chairman of the Western States Regional Manpower Advisory Committee to the two Secretaries. He was also a member of President Johnson's task force on Occupational Training in Industry.

Mr. Boynton's great interest in education includes two years as vice chairman of the Junior College Advisory Panel to the California State Board of Education, several years as vice president of the Northern California Industry Education Council and present membership in the Board of Directors, West Coast, International Institute of Education, the National Board of Overseers, Lewis and Clark College and the Education Committee, California Chamber of Commerce. He wrote with two others a national assessment of Career Guidance that was published by the U.S. Department of Labor.

In addition to church and civic activities Mr. Boynton is a member of the University Club of San Francisco, the Los Angeles Athletic Club, Sigma Alpha Epsilon and the Commonwealth Club, San Francisco. He lives in Menlo Park, California with his wife, Helen.

Contents

Preface

One dreary morning in January, 1933, the telephone began ringing in the San Francisco office of A. P. Giannini, founder of Bank of America. Giannini turned from a desk littered with reports and papers and lifted the receiver of the jangling instrument.

An associate at one of Bank of America's Sacramento branches was on the other end of the line. Giannini listened for a moment then interrupted briskly. "Keep paying out cash—I'll be there in an hour with five million dollars!"

Earlier that day a large Sacramento bank had failed to open—and now depositors, in a state of panic, were rushing to every bank in the city, trying to withdraw their funds.

Before the phone call was a half hour old, one of Giannini's trusted aids was winging toward Sacramento at nearly two hundred miles an hour. Beside him in the plane lay seven mail sacks, bulging with five million dollars in currency. At the same moment Giannini and another aide were heading toward Sacramento in a private automobile.

The money was rushed from the airport to the bank's Sacramento main office. Long lines of nervous customers, each hoping the cash would hold out until he reached the teller window, jammed the bank's lobby. Through this throng strode Giannini, accompanied by ten policemen and seven detectives toting the precious mail sacks. Then, in full view of the crowd, Giannini cracked open three of the sacks and laid their contents out in the open. He told the depositors there was plenty of money—that all the banks in town were perfectly safe.

The sight of those stacks of crisp bills and the confident tone of Giannini's words immediately eased the tension in the overfilled lobby. Reassured customers, with one last look at more money than most of them would ever see again, began filing out of the bank and back home. Within two hours there was no vestige of a run on any bank in the city.

This story is one of the earliest—and most dramatic—demonstrations of the virtue of American *branch* banking. Until the 1900's such a system had not gained much of a foothold in the United States. It had been practiced for many years in Canada and other countries, but *unit* banking—individual financial institutions with only one office, one location—had remained by far the predominant system in this nation.

Then in 1908, one year after a serious recession had caused a number of banks throughout the country to close, Giannini attended a banker's conference and listened to Lyman J. Gage, a former Secretary of the Treasury, argue for branch banking as a stabilizing force in the economy. He cited "the utter lack of unity and mutual cohesion among the units composing the ten thousand or more banks in the United States. Always in competition, at the moment of stress or strain, they fly apart, *each determined to save itself*."

Giannini may well have remembered these words on that day in 1933 when, by using funds from his stable and unthreatened branches in San Francisco, he averted banking disaster in Sacramento. Had the Sacramento banks been entirely on their own, they might not have withstood the run.

There was another persuasive speaker at the 1908 conference: Woodrow Wilson, then president of Princeton University. The bank panic of 1907 had illustrated clearly that the banking industry in the United States was disorganized and chaotic, and served well only the few citizens who were fortunate enough to dwell near the nation's financial centers. Wilson suggested branch banking as a remedy which would "put the resources of the rich banks of the country at the disposal of the whole countrysides to whose merchants and farmers only a restricted and local credit is now open. . . ."

This idea had been gaining popularity in the United States, and it aroused Giannini's interest. He traveled through Canada, studying their successful branch system, and decided that here was a way he could bring the services of his bank to all the people of California.

Two years later he opened an office in San Jose. This was his first branch outside of San Francisco. His brother, Dr. A. H. Giannini, outlined the operating philosophy underlying the new office in San Jose: "This does not mean that San Jose coin will be taken away to San Francisco, but that San Francisco coin will be brought into San Jose."

By practicing this principle throughout his lifetime, Giannini made the Bank of America's resources available to the smallest businessman in the most remote area of the state. Today the bank has more than 1000 community offices in California, in addition to branches and representative offices located around the world. And nearly every one of these branches provides the entire range of our 128 banking services to its customers. Behind our smallest branch in a wilderness area of California stands the strength, knowledge, and experience of the biggest bank in the world: Bank of America.

In writing this book, then, branch banking will be my

frame of reference. This is the area in which I found the greatest opportunity and built my career. This is the area I am most familiar with. But it also seems to me that, from the viewpoint of a young career-seeker, branch banking offers a combination of the advantages and opportunities found in both small and large unit banks.

In a large bank, for example, there is the opportunity to specialize. For the ambitious and talented, competition with other able young people offers a stimulating challenge. The small bank, on the other hand, offers greater personal prestige for the banker in his own community. He is friend and advisor to his fellow residents and businessmen. Also, the officer of a small bank may have a greater personal impact upon his institution. In many instances he can influence the bank's policies, philosophy, public image, and even its physical appearance more significantly.

The branch system combines the best aspects of both small and large banks. For those interested in pure banking experience, there is an opportunity to gain a wide range of knowledge by working in branches in various locations. It is therefore possible for a young officer to develop all of his abilities and interests to a high degree by transferring to branches with different community characteristics. He can attain a high level of independence and prestige in the particular branch in which he operates. At the same time he can rely upon his organization's specialists to help him with problems outside his area of competence. The ambitious officer has the choice of striving for the highest possible branch position or moving into the administrative departments. He can even combine the two types of careers.

Those of you who are now about to embark upon your careers are indeed fortunate. Never in history have young men and women had so great an opportunity to follow their own talents, skills, and preferences in shaping their futures as they have in modern America. Never before have so many had the opportunity to acquire the education needed for the career they want. And never before have so many varied and challenging types of work been open to young people.

R. E. B.
June 1, 1975
San Francisco, California

YOUR FUTURE IN BANKING

CHAPTER I

Getting in on the Ground Floor

Today's banking industry is 4,000 years young. Gone forever is the melodramatic stereotype of old-fashioned bankers: aloof, fish-eyed men perpetually foreclosing mortgage on penniless and innocent fair-haired maidens. Now if you say "I'm going to see my banker," it is as natural as making an appointment with a doctor or consulting your lawyer about a legal question.

Gone too is the notion that banks and bank services are available only to the wealthy few. Just about everyone nowadays has a bank account. And most people depend upon their local bank to help them manage money in a hundred different ways—because banks are no longer simply places to put valuables for safekeeping or to get a loan when you are short of funds.

Even the building in which the modern bank operates is different from the old. Few banks are constructing the imposing Greek temples once thought to convey an aura of security and conservatism. Today's bank often is housed in a pleasant contemporary structure which symbolizes its role as a progressive, well-integrated part of the community it serves.

The fact is that though banks have been around longer than almost any other industry, they were for centuries painfully slow in developing their potential. Only with the advent of the 1900's did the full scope of banking opportunities begin to be explored. And as bankers have adopted new attitudes toward their role in serving the public, old and outmoded practices have been cast off and an entirely new brand of banking has emerged.

A New Role

One of the first rumblings of change came from San Francisco two years before the great earthquake and fire of 1906. That was in 1904, the year A. P. Giannini founded an institution that would one day become Bank of America.

"This is a bank for the little fellow," boomed Giannini and the echo of those words continued to resound across the expanses of California long after the great San Francisco earthquake was a matter of concern only to historians and geologists.

At first Giannini was referring primarily to members of the city's Italian community—honest, hard-working people whose dreams far outweighed their pocketbooks. These men were used to keeping their savings in cookie jars and mattresses, and borrowing money from friends who had been more thrifty than they. Most had never been inside a bank.

By tailoring bank services to the specific needs of these people, Giannini argued, and by making them the stockholders, the actual owners of Bank of America, they would automatically come to trust and depend upon the institution. He was right. In a short while Bank of America was providing money and services to the millions of "little fellows" in cities throughout the state of California.

What Giannini had proposed and done was amazing in its simplicity. Banks traditionally served people and enterprises that had already amassed a good deal of money. Wealth was the measure of trustworthiness. Giannini shifted the emphasis to character. He was willing to bank on people if they seemed honest and industrious.

More importantly he felt it was the bank's *responsibility* to help these people better their condition. By imposing this sense of social responsibility upon his financial institution, Giannini, along with other farsighted commercial leaders, cast an entirely new role for American business and opened broad new vistas of opportunity.

Once the initial step was taken, it was not difficult for banks to extend this sense of responsibility toward industries, communities, even entire populations. For banks occupy a unique and catalytic position in any free society. They are guardians of the public wealth. With them rests the responsibility of amassing idle funds and channeling them into productive, beneficial projects. And without banks it is unlikely we could enjoy many of the conveniences we do today.

How many people, for example, would own automobiles today if it were not for the availability of bank credit? How many could afford their own homes and furniture? How many would go to college? The list is endless.

On a larger scale, consider some of the public benefits we enjoy because a bank acted in good faith at a crucial point in history. There is a story which describes how A. P. Giannini was visited one day in 1932 by a famous engineer named Joseph B. Strauss. Strauss was sponsoring a daring project that for nearly nineteen years had been bedeviled and delayed by petty politics, false rumor, and raging public controversy. The project had been initiated by M. M. O'Shaughnessy, Chief Engineer of San Francisco. He had, years earlier, designed a bridge to close the mile-wide gap at the entrance to the San Francisco Bay.

The physical obstacles to such a plan were in themselves almost overwhelming. Erratic tides and currents, sweeping winds, and water of such a depth that the bridge could not be anchored at the center of the bay's mouth called for an ingenious design solution. But even when that solution was found, the project could not proceed. The approach to the bridge, on both sides of the bay, would have to traverse government military property. The War Department pointed out that a bombproof powder magazine control, a new rifle range, a rifle station for coast defense guns, officers' quarters, repair shops, and more than 10,000 feet of elevated viaduct to carry traffic over the military reservation would have to be constructed. Shipping interests were also less than enthusiastic about the plan and demanded a hundred more feet of high-tide clearance than the Brooklyn Bridge offered.

When at last the bridge gained approval through a public vote it was thrown again into disrepute by the story that the base rock at the end of the pier was "as mushy as quicksand." Moreover, a prominent geologist reported that the pier base rested upon a structural fault.

By the time all these obstructions had been cleared from the path of the bridge, the country had entered a period of hard times and tight money control. The government's Reconstruction Finance Corporation had allotted its entire appropriation to the San Francisco–Oakland Bay Bridge. And there was no market for the $6,000,000 in bonds that must be sold to finance the new bridge.

This was the story Strauss recounted to Giannini on that day in 1932. Giannini's decision was swift and to the point.

"We'll take the bonds."

Thus today, thousands of motorists in the San Francisco area enjoy the easy accessibility of a downtown urban working area to outlying, pleasant residential districts. Each day thousands of commuters pour across the bridge carrying workers to and from their jobs. More importantly, America has a rich addition to her architectural heritage: the Golden Gate Bridge—a sweeping span of concrete and steel that is known and admired by peoples of all nations. Yet this achievement might have died on the drawing board had it not been for the courage and farsightedness of a banker with a commitment to public welfare.

Today the history books, the cities and homes we live in are filled with similar examples. Every time you see a new shopping center, a modern skyscraper, a well-equipped park or playground, a vast industrial complex, you can be certain that some bank played an important role in its development.

Banks Go Retail

The liberalizing of the banker's view of himself and his role brought profound changes in his methods of doing business. For years it had been "beneath his dignity" to actually go out and solicit business. Let people come to him when they need help. Financial service was not something you sold in the manner you might market a used car, a hairbrush or a brand of breakfast food.

About the only occasion on which banks used advertising, for example, was to publish a periodic statement of condition in the newspaper. Therefore, when A. P. Giannini began to open branches in Los Angeles, fellow bankers were astounded to see a large advertisement appear in the local newspapers listing the names of the directors and advisory board members of the new bank. Astounded, but quick to respond!

Five days later a competitor bank ran an ad listing its board of directors—and including the provocative rejoiner, "You will note that practically all have been residents of Los Angeles for over twenty years."

Other California banks did not hesitate to follow suit. Security Trust announced in the newspaper that "THIS BANK PAYS THE HIGHEST RATE OF INTEREST CONSISTENT WITH SAFE CONSERVATIVE BANKING." Giannini retorted with this sharp headline: "SAFETY AND 4% AND NOTE THAT THE MATTER OF INTEREST COMES SECOND." So the battle was on and banks found themselves a powerful new sales tool—advertising.

Bankers also discovered that to survive they could no longer stay glued to desks in cool, formal, marble-trimmed offices. Competition was too hot. To sell the public on their bank, on their services, they would have to get out and meet people—become more active in civic affairs, make regular business calls on old customers, and seek out potential new customers.

Marketing Money

By adopting the view that all income and social groups are entitled to bank facilities, bankers had greatly widened the market for their services. Advertising and aggressive sales policies had done much to make that market understand the usefulness of banks. Now came the third step in the process: second-guessing the public's financial needs and devising services to meet them.

In very simple terms this is called marketing, and now banks entered the field with enthusiasm and imagination.

Someone noted that when people traveled long distances they preferred not to carry large amounts of cash with them, fearing either loss or theft. On the other hand when in strange territory, they were unable to cash personal checks. The result: travelers cheques. Here was a medium as good as cash *as soon as signed* by the owner. Anyone almost any place in the world would accept them. If they were stolen or lost before being signed, the owner could quickly get his money back from the bank where he purchased them.

Someone else realized that many older people of substantial means had either never made wills or had no one to administer their estates after death. Other people with large amounts of money had either insufficient time or lacked specialized knowledge to watch over it day by day. They would have preferred to turn it over to some expert. Thus the concept of trust administration was born to help people manage their money.

And so the list of services grew until it came to include such diverse items as safe deposit facilities, money orders and cashiers checks, special installment loan classifications, foreign exchange, bond investment, and a variety of others.

Enter Technology

The practical adding machine came into bank use late in the 1800's. A hundred years earlier the industrial revolution had begun, but most of the new tools and machinery developed had only an indirect effect on bank operations. Few of the products of the revolution were applied to the actual operating procedures of financial institutions. Banks remained largely unmechanized, depending on only adding machines to help them with their accounting and paper work.

All that is past history, because about fifteen years ago man began to use electronic computers for processing information. The impact of this new tool on banking methods was indeed profound.

Let me illustrate with a commonly accepted rule: if *one part* of a situation changes by one thousand per cent the entire situation becomes significantly different.

For example, let's look at what happened when new and faster tools became available in the past—tools whose speed represented an increase of 1,000 or more percent. One tool is transportation. A man who has only a beast of burden for transportation travels around five miles an hour. His food cannot be transported very far; his society is primarily agricultural.

When machines became available for transportation, a man could go roughly fifty miles an hour—an increase of 1,000 percent. And, as a result, his whole living and working situation could change too. Now he could work in a central city, live in outlying suburbs, and have remote agricultural and recreational areas within easy travel time.

A jet airplane represents another tenfold increase in speed of transportation. The man who uses jet airplanes regularly has an entire nation, or the world as his sphere of operations. Once again, there has been a fundamental change because of an increase of 1,000 percent in the speed of a tool—transportation.

Calculating and accounting are basic activities of banking. Imagine the speed of one person using an adding machine. An electronic computer can carry out each calculation 100,000 times faster.

100,000 times faster! That is like saying the bank manager who has the work of one employee available to him now, with a computer, has the potential production of 100,000 employees.

Today nearly every bank in our country is serviced in some way by computers. Bank accounts of all types are serviced with a speed and accuracy unheard of only a few decades ago. Moreover, the range and variety of financial services available to the public has increased dramatically with the advent of electronic accounting.

A bank is now capable of handling an entire payroll for a company: from basic data supplied by the employer, the bank produces payroll checks, tax reports, and all necessary records. If you're a doctor or lawyer and do not want to be bothered with sending out monthly statements, your bank can do it for you. Shortly after Bank of America converted to electronic accounting, we offered credit cards to our customers. More than three million Californians enjoy the convenience of a BankAmericard—an all-purpose family credit card that provides an automatic charge account at thousands of retail stores, service businesses, and professional offices throughout the state.

The transition to automated banking, however, has not always been a smooth one. There have been technical problems; and there has been resistance among some who feel these new machines represent a threat to their jobs. But are these electronic computers, these data processing devices and techniques really a threat—or are they one of the most magnificent opportunities ever presented to banking?

Are they the "magic brains" of the comic strips and cartoons, soon to usurp our abilities to think, to plan, to decide; or are they marvelous new tools that will truly enhance the status of the individual, giving him greater ability to use his distinctly human capabilities?

It depends on the man. There was once a fellow with a shovel in his hand who looked at a bulldozer and gave up in defeat. There was another man who reached for the controls and began to move a mountain!

With this new tool, with aggressive sales attitudes, and with a strong and continuing desire to serve the public's best interest, banks are going to be moving some pretty impressive mountains in the years ahead.

Bank of Tomorrow

Free from drudgery and paper work, and provided with more information for decision and planning, bankers in the future will be even more effective in serving the public. But their primary task and satisfaction will continue to be the development and maintenance of the highest levels of personal service to those with financial needs. They will become, even more than they are today, financial advisors to their customers, suggesting total service tailored to individual requirements.

This then is what the future holds in store for the young man or woman seeking a career in today's banking industry. We stand on the threshold of a bold new era in financial services. The changes that are yet to come will be bigger, faster, and even more dramatic than those that have already occurred.

To help formulate and guide those changes banking needs youth, imagination, resourcefulness, and determination. It needs people who are looking for a career in an industry that is really just beginning to grow—where the best is still ahead—where you can get in on the ground floor.

CHAPTER II

Who Says a Good Banker Has to Be Dull?

I remember a young fellow who several years ago came to our bank with an outstanding college record. He was intelligent and able. He took hold of his assigned duties and became proficient at them. His superior was asked to try him in new and more responsible work, to have him make decisions, to watch his relations with his fellow workers, looking particularly for leadership ability. We wanted to learn in which area he showed the greatest interest and skill so we could determine the right moment to move him upward.

But we were badly disappointed. This man showed little inclination to extend himself into new areas of responsibility or to develop new skills. His attitude toward his co-employees was, "You do your work; I'll do mine." We felt perhaps he did not find his work challenging enough or that there was a personality conflict in his department. We tried him in other posts. But in each one he showed interest only in performing his assigned duties satisfactorily. Today, he holds a position only slightly higher than that for which he was hired.

Perhaps this man is satisfied with his progress—but I doubt

it. It must be disheartening for him to watch the rise of other employees; some have become his superiors, others have bypassed him and gone into entirely new areas. Paradoxically, he is every bit as able, and in some cases even more talented than they are. But they have tried harder to learn and grow.

Bureaucrat Means Beaten

The young man I've been speaking of is well on his way to becoming what some people call a bureaucrat. The bureaucrat is one of the more unfortunate products of our age and he exists at all levels in most companies.

He doesn't believe in knocking himself out working, although strangely enough he may often put in long hours. When he first came to work his greatest interest was security. It still is.

The bureaucrat rarely thinks about profit, though it is profit that pays his wage. He seldom examines seriously the caliber of service he is providing his customers. He rarely, if ever, considers ultimate goals and therefore he manages by system rather than objective. He assumes that time and seniority will provide advancement in position, in title and in salary; competition is merely something to which he pays occasional lip service.

Bureaucrats are, in fact, "systems people" through and through. No new ideas for them. No desire to cut red tape and get the job done. Their philosophy of life and work can be summed up as a series of narrow absolutes: never take chances, never support an unpopular cause, never take personal responsibility. Always get a "committee" decision; always make sure that no one can blame you for a mistake; always play it safe; always dodge the tough ones.

Bureaucrats often think they are good company people. Some of them even fool themselves into thinking they are happy. But in truth, such people are barely alive. They live in a dreary half world, knowing neither the deep satisfaction of well-earned victory nor the bitter disappointment of defeat after a hard fight. A person who has not experienced both has not done much with his or her life. Bureaucrats never will because they are beaten before they begin.

So whatever career you embark upon, beware of bureaucracy. A sudden setback, a series of discouragements, a natural distaste for your work—any of these elements can sap you of your energy and courage and turn you into a hyper-cautious, faltering, ineffective bureaucrat overnight. And it can happen at any point in your life—whether you are age fifty or just starting out.

An old geometric postulate describes a straight line as the shortest distance between two points. You stand at one point today. From here, you will set out for the second point: your ultimate career goal. It is important that you decide upon and keep this goal in mind in everything you do from now on. Take each new experience and elements and information which will move you forward toward your career goal.

In this way you will avoid much frustration and disappointment, as well as wasted years. And you will be helping yourself to guard against the ever present danger of bureaucracy.

Doing What Comes Naturally

Your natural aptitudes—the things you enjoy doing and do well—should be instrumental in helping pinpoint the field in which you will have the best chance of success. A great deal of your life will be spent working at your career; eight hours a day, or forty hours a week will be the bare minimum. To attain success, you must devote much more time to your work than is required. There will be the hours you spend at your desk, performing routine tasks. But when you leave your desk, your job will go with you. Many "off duty" hours will be spent thinking about new approaches to problems, developing new ideas to improve your own performance and that of others about you, and learning more about your field. In order that you may live with your work constructively, it is vital that you truly enjoy your profession and find it stimulating.

I recall the words of the founder of Bank of America, A. P. Giannini. He once said of his work: "A lot of people you and I know get through their jobs every day so they can get out to something else. Their jobs are a more or less disagreeable necessity to their lives; they get through them as best they can so as to go to what they like better. Some of them are thinking of home and dinner, others want to get up to the club, get out in the car, play some game. Well, this is my game. I get more fun out of doing just what I'm doing here than anything else I know."

Finding true pleasure in your work, then, is the cornerstone of success. But there are other qualifications with which you build from this foundation.

Striking a Balance

There was a time when a banking career required little more than honesty, accuracy, and good judgment. These attributes still rate pretty high on any list of job qualifications. After all, banking is a public trust. As a member of the profession you are entrusted with other people's wealth; you are expected to keep an accurate account of it; you are relied upon for sound advice in financial matters.

But honesty, accuracy, and good judgment by no means constitute a complete formula for success in today's banking industry. The banker who views present and prospective customers only in terms of balance sheets and financial statements is now as out-of-date as the hand-cranked phonograph.

At one time or another in the course of life, nearly everyone—young and old, rich and poor—seeks the advice and assistance of his banker. The banker, in turn, likes the people with whom he deals and enjoys helping them.

A great deal of his satisfaction must come from helping others build, because this is the nature of the modern banker's business. Young married people seek counsel in buying and furnishing their first home, in purchasing a new car, in making financial plans for their family's education.

Businessmen seek advice on how to make more efficient use of capital, how best to expand production, how to open new markets for their products.

People in their middle years bring in their life savings and ask for help in making investments and estate plans, which will give them income and security in their later years and which will assure that the benefits of their life's work will be passed on most equitably to their heirs.

Gaining the respect and confidence of so many diverse groups is no mean task. You must be knowledgeable in each of the fields most closely allied with their interests. This means understanding agriculture as well as food processing and packing; retailing as well as wholesaling; capital investment as well as personal money management; the intricacies of running a giant corporation as well as the difficulties in sustaining a small, one-man enterprise.

You must also be willing to accept time-consuming civic responsibilities, to demonstrate your capacity for leadership and your interest in the welfare of others by participating actively in community affairs.

You should keep abreast of the news. Know who our elected officials are and what is going on in the government; where international trouble spots are; what national events are currently making the headlines. But keep track of other things too. Know who wrote the latest best seller, what the stock market did yesterday, who's playing in the World Series—remember, as a banker you will be serving diverse groups of people and the more well informed you are, the more confidence they will place in you.

Of course, even if you are the best informed person in the world, it will be of no avail unless you can communicate. It is extremely important for any business or professional person, but especially for a banker, to be articulate. Some people are naturally gifted in this respect, but the majority of us must acquire it and must work constantly to perfect it.

In banking, it is important because of the complicated nature of various operations which must be explained to our customers. People are suspicious of that which they do not understand. But once procedures and the reasons behind them are explained clearly and logically, people will usually accept them.

The ability to communicate clearly information with which you are extremely familiar to those who have no concept of your operation is an art which must not be underestimated. Unless bankers master this art, they cannot adequately explain the value of a service to the customer who needs it. In other words, they are not serving the public as well as they might.

Finally, to gain the respect of the people you serve *and* the institution you work for, you must develop a high degree of technical competence in the mechanics of your field—banking. Know the principles of accounting and bookkeeping, learn what types of collateral are acceptable, how interest rates are determined, what servicing a checking account involves, the manner in which loans are documented. This knowledge will come naturally if you find your work interesting and challenging—willingness to learn and improve is one of the elements sought by administrators who select young people to be moved into more responsible jobs.

As your competence grows and your experience broadens, you must acquire administrative ability: the ability to direct and work through others to get the job done. Many competent young people who fail to develop the essential tools of leadership are bypassed in the promotion process. And no matter how stimulating they have found their work in the past, the knowledge that they have come to a dead end in their careers dulls their interest and sense of fulfillment.

So the business of becoming a successful banker is somewhat like putting together a patchwork quilt. Only after sewing into your character an immense variety of attitudes, interests, and talents, and striking a harmonious balance among them will you emerge fully qualified to serve the banking needs of today's society.

Glamour Is Only Skin-Deep

You may have heard the story about the three men who were once asked what their occupations were. The first reported he worked in the movie business. The second declared he did detective work. And the third said he was an electrician.

It sounded as though the first two had rather glamorous jobs. As it turned out one was a janitor in the local motion picture theatre and the other was a field representative for a marketing research organization. He spent his days going from house to house, ringing doorbells, and asking people what they thought of a new brand of toothpaste.

The third fellow—the "electrician"—was president of one of the largest power and light companies in the country. He earned $100,000 a year, was responsible for thousands of employees and to thousands of stockholders, occupied a trusteeship on the board of the local college, had a Ph.D. in economics and was one of the leading citizens in his state and community.

So don't be fooled by glamorous-sounding jobs. And don't expect too much, too fast. Recruiters for industry and other personnel people comment that many job applicants fail to seriously consider the future of a position which is offered to them. They want success, and the glamour which attaches to apparent success immediately, and they fail to give adequate consideration to whether or not there is opportunity to grow and advance.

Jobs which offer immediate glamour and excitement too often grow routine and dull after a time, when employees begin to realize they are not being offered the training or experience to advance into more challenging positions. At this point, after a number of valuable years have been wasted, they find they must begin again to build careers solidly based on training, experience, and proven competence.

Be Uncommon

I wrote earlier about the bureaucrat and dangers of following his code of survival. There is in today's commercial world, however, an opposite type of person and whether you enter banking or some other field, this is the person you should strive to emulate.

Back in World War II it was said of the marines on Guadalcanal that "uncommon valor was a common virtue." Our second type of person is something like that. He or she wasn't born with the singular genius which characterizes a very few people in each generation—the Benjamin Franklins, the Clara Bartons, the Madame Curies, the Henry Fords—and the A. P. Gianninis. Whether born in a mansion or a slum, he or she was born a common person in this sense, and yet, each made himself or herself into an uncommon person.

What are uncommon persons like?

They are about the opposite of the bureaucrat. They dream big dreams, but they are no idle dreamers. They set their imaginations and their minds free to create change. They know that their security is in themselves. They are thoroughly profit-oriented. They know in every fiber of their being that "profit" is a result which every business person must seek and from which our country and all its citizens grow and prosper. They are big enough and broad enough to understand the significance of profit to the entire fabric of our social system.

Uncommon people manage by objectives. They look to where they want to go and choose the best method to get there. They aren't bound solely by system and precedent and they thrive on new ideas and new methods. They are at home with change. They are impatient with red tape and infuriated by "make work." They are willing to fight for what they believe to be right. They are willing to dare, to take responsibility, to support an unpopular cause. They make their own decisions. They know they are going to make mistakes but they know also that those who never make mistakes miss the opportunities that lead to success.

Uncommon people are conformists in the best sense of the word. They are polite. They are respectful of their associates. They are genuinely interested in the people with whom they work. They like to work with them and to help them. They are friendly beyond the superficialities that sometimes passes as friendliness, because they recognize the inherent worth of other people. Uncommon people are conformists in their virtues. They believe in some things that our age rails against. They believe in hard work. They believe in personal integrity. They believe our ingenuity can conquer our problems. They are proud of their heritage as Americans. They are proud of success. They are proud of their families. They are proud of the economic system of which they are a part.

But uncommon people are notably nonconformists in the finest sense of that badly abused term.

They are nonconformists in the world of ideas.

They are nonconformists when it comes to hidebound belief in any given system of doing things.

They are nonconformists because they dare to look for a better way. They are always bothered by the imperfections they see all about them and within themselves.

To paraphrase George Bernard Shaw: Conformists try to adjust to the world as they find it. Nonconformists try to adjust the world for the better. Hence progress depends on nonconformists—the uncommon people.

These are the sorts of people to whom the doors of industry, business and especially banking always will be wide open. These are the sort of people who will be guiding these enterprises in the exciting years ahead.

CHAPTER III

Something for Everyone

There's more to an iceberg than meets the eye, almost seven times more as a matter of fact. That tiny pyramid you see above the water's surface is supported from beneath by a massive ice structure, hundreds of tons in weight and completely hidden from view.

The same might be said for a dramatic play. For every actor you see on the stage there are at least seven other people behind the scenes who play a crucial, but silent role in the performance. Without directors, producers, costume and set designers, spotlight and properties crews, ushers, and stage managers, the curtain would never go up.

What holds for icebergs and theatrical productions also holds for large unit banks and branch bank systems. Today's big banks provide so many varied services and cover such broad geographic areas that they must depend upon highly specialized technicians to direct and supervise highly specialized functions.

In a unit bank these technicians may continue to deal directly with the public—but they will handle only those transactions which fall within their particular field of specialization. In a branch system, the experts may be assigned to an administrative headquarters where they seldom come in actual contact with customers. However, they will be readily available to aid, advise, and supervise in instances where the case presents problems beyond the average branch banker's knowledge or authority.

For a young career-seeker, the important thing to remember is this: *Banking is a profession where there is need for a wide range of special aptitudes and interests.* As you read this chapter you'll find that people with backgrounds in finance, business, investment, law, economics, marketing, mathematics, and the creative arts all play an important role in the operation of a modern bank.

The Lending Art

Young people interested in learning about finance, budgeting, and how to help others acquire the goods or security they want and need will find lending a fertile area in which to fulfill these interests. Naturally, certain standard attributes are required of all personnel before they are qualified to make responsible loans. They must be able interviewers and good judges of character. They must be cautious and thorough yet imaginative and resourceful. They must be familiar with the general requirements of loan documentation and the overall legal aspects of negotiable instruments. They should have some knowledge of accounting and of financial statement analysis.

Beyond this, making effective loans is a matter of experience and specialization. The more you know about the particular field in which the loan applies, the better chance you will have of making a wise decision. For example, through installment lending, banks help consumers and small businessmen attain advantages they might otherwise be unable to afford. Each week, a bank officer helps dozens of customers budget their incomes and acquire more necessities and comforts for themselves, their families, and their firms by educating them in the basic principles of money-handling and by tailoring loans to fit their specific needs.

Take the case of the young fellow, twenty-one years old, who one day climbed into his jalopy and headed out of Los Angeles for Tulare, California. When he arrived, he banked his little nest egg at our Tulare office of Bank of America and went into business—making tortillas to sell to residents who enjoyed Mexican food. Before long, he was in our local branch again, asking for and receiving a personal loan to enlarge his little business. That was fifteen years ago. Today the young man owns and manages a factory that turns out tortillas in assembly-line numbers. The thin, flat cakes are no longer made by hand, for the machine he invented and had financed by a business term loan speeds them out with automated efficiency that assures quality.

Another man who financed his daughter's education with an installment loan wrote us: "My daughter spent one year at the University of California in Berkeley and then went to New York City, where she was graduated from the Neighborhood Playhouse, a famous school of drama. She also studied voice with a famous singer in the Metropolitan Opera Company. She may someday be a well-known singer herself, and this was all made possible because, four years ago, you thoughtfully suggested to me a Studyplan loan. The cost of keeping my daughter in New York City, paying the tuition at the Playhouse, and for the voice lessons was staggering and couldn't have been accomplished without your help . . ."

In this day of greater savings and more leisure, some of

our customers use installment loans to pay for pleasure boats and even private planes. A grandmother, for instance, came into one of our branches last year and headed straight for the installment lending department. "I want to buy a plane," she said, with a no-nonsense gleam in her eye. "I'm learning to fly and after I get my license and log enough hours, I plan to teach my grandson in my own plane!" (Her credit was good, and she did just that.)

In many cases, you don't even have to visit your bank to receive an installment loan. You will find that the dealer or store from whom you purchase a product or service will have on hand all the papers and information necessary to extend you a loan. But the actual processing of those papers; the responsibility for approving and maintaining the loan; the real source of the money that pays for the purchase is a bank. By far the largest share of this financing activity involves automobiles, but it also includes a wide variety of other items, such as appliances, mobile homes, home improvements, and professional services like dental and hospital bills. Also covered is income-producing equipment such as trucks and industrial and farm machinery. Many a small automobile business has grown into a big dealership, selling hundreds of cars a year, with the help of installment financing. More than one trucking system has started out with a single vehicle and, with installment financing, expanded into a sizable and profitable business.

Dealers and distributors are also financed for "working capital" purposes through loans on certain goods in inventory such as automobiles, stoves, and refrigerators. The dealer pledges the goods on hand as security and in return receives from the bank funds to meet the cost of carrying such inventory items. Dealers may also pledge their "accounts receivable"—goods and services sold and delivered to customers but for which payment has not yet been received.

Due to the variety of people, products, services, and conditions involved in installment financing, it is a field that offers the banker great opportunities for specialization. The same opportunities can be found in the field of corporate or commercial finance. Knowledge and counsel in this field are needed to enable industries of all sizes and types to build and grow. Within this framework a broad interest in the inner mechanics of business and a variety of special interests—from electronics to transportation to the arts—is valuable. Those with an interest in agricultural economics are needed particularly in branch banking systems or in rural unit banks. With knowledge and experience in this field, a bank lending officer can help farmers increase the size, productivity, and efficiency of their lands through better equipment and horticultural practices. Real estate presents still another area of opportunity for the lending specialist. Banks lend money to buy or build homes, apartment houses, stores, factories, and other types of property. It takes an expert to unravel the complex variety of tax and zoning laws, building codes, and insurance requirements that accompany the granting of a real estate loan.

In some instances it is not the purpose for which a loan is being used, but the method of securing it that demands the attention of a specialist. Such is the case with commodity loans. These loans are normally made to producers, processors, manufacturers, distributors and dealers—in return for cash they pledge as security all types of readily marketable commodities, raw materials and, in some instances, finished goods. It is imperative that lending officers in this field be thoroughly familiar with each of the industries and the economic pressures and outlooks for each of the products used as security.

For example, a bank officer may be a specialist in such merchandise as dried fruits, frozen foods, nuts, olives, and canned goods. Another may have the responsibility of lending money on wine, beans, coffee, tobacco, chemicals, and steel. Each must know the quantities and the markets for these products as produced throughout the world and the factors surrounding their procurement, processing, and selling.

These, then, are a few of the areas in which a lending officer can specialize. However, there is no set pattern for developing lending experts. Experience counts a great deal and so does maturity and judgment. For these reasons, most loan specialists are in their late thirties or above, who have had an opportunity to develop a high degree of competence in their field.

It is likely that the demand for this sort of person will remain strong in years ahead. First of all, loans are one of the prime sources of bank income—and profit. The bank that develops lending experts increases its ability to make the soundest loans possible and to provide customers with the highest caliber of service. Finally, as our commercial society grows increasingly complex, as new techniques and procedures emerge, the general lending field will become even broader, offering more and more potential for the banker who wants to specialize.

How Much and How Safe?

There are a number of other activities coincident to the lending process that require an expert's touch. Appraising and credit investigation are two good examples.

When a bank makes a secured loan, an appraiser is usually needed to verify the existence and determine the value of the collateral. The work varies from day to day; counting sheep, cattle or pigs, estimating the value for loan purposes of new homes or those being sold to new owners, or making a complete safety check of the rides and concessions at an amusement park. A construction job could require climbing along narrow steel girders to make an inspection for a progress payment, and an agricultural assignment might necessitate tramping across acres of farmland in order to look over a crop of corn.

Another category of appraisals falls properly into neither the agricultural or urban group. These might be called the "off beat" appraisals. For example, Bank of America's appraisal department was once asked to evaluate, from plans and blueprints, a "shipwreck" to be constructed off the coast of Northern California and used as a maritime museum.

Because of the technical problems involved, appraisal departments frequently rely on people with special training. Engineers may be consulted to develop current cost information to guide the field staff in determining the cost of a structure and the procedures for making progress inspections. Geologists or people with a similar background may be needed to counsel the department on such technical points as earth slide, soil conditions, earthquake precautions, and other special problems.

On the other hand, many of the appraisers in our department have either spent a good many years working in branches or have had extensive orientation programs in the branch system to familiarize them with operations and special problems. Many are sent to special short courses at nearby educational institutions. They also keep abreast of developments in their fields by participating actively in professional organizations.

In some ways it is indeed strange work for bankers, but appraisers perform an important banking service. They act as the "eyes of the bank" in reviewing the collateral for many types of loans.

Another important prerequisite to making a sound loan is thorough credit investigation. Although those who work in bank credit departments don't usually consider magnifying glasses and bloodhounds as standard office equipment, when it comes to ferreting out credit information they can match the old master Sherlock Holmes anytime.

As its name suggests, the credit department reviews and analyzes the bank's loans to help prevent losses. Department members carefully scrutinize a multitude of forms and reports to make sure all loans conform to bank policy, are legal, and are generally sound extensions of credit. Another important function is checking the credit standing of a customer before a loan is made. Still another function is answering valid credit inquiries about certain customers.

As one of our credit officers puts it, "This section acts almost like a clearing house for any correspondence that mentions credit. It doesn't take long for our people to become experts on every type of domestic problem that could result in a late loan payment."

They also learn how to handle inquiries that are more concerned with hearts and flowers than finance. For example, one inquiry was recently received from an overseas bank. It seems a foreign exchange student in this country had fallen in love with a young American boy. The student's parents, customers of the overseas bank, wanted a dossier on the young man before giving their blessings to the match.

What kind of background does a credit officer need to handle all of these diverse duties? A good, solid knowledge of banking and the myriad related subjects such as commercial law, negotiable instruments, and accounting all mixed together with patience, persistence, and experience.

Managing Money and Securities

A bank's cashier's department is responsible for maintaining accounting records and investments in securities. The latter involves a large share of the bank's total resources. Staff members must be experts in a wide variety of specialities. They must be equipped to manage the central problem confronting every banker.

Depositors leave their money with a bank for safety, convenience, and reward. Money is always flowing in and out of the bank so the deposit supply is constantly changing. On the one hand, depositors expect to be able to get their money when they want it—often on demand. Because the banker must always be ready to satisfy these demands, an adequate supply of cash must always be available. On the other hand, since idle cash earns nothing, a profitable bank must try to keep as large a part of deposits as possible working at interest to earn income.

The cashier's department manages this flow of funds and makes plans and forecasts to cope with the ever changing supply and demand for deposit funds. A part of the bank's deposits are held in the form of cash in the branches to meet withdrawal needs. The surplus is invested or loaned. Part of this surplus is maintained in very short-term loans or securities that can be converted quickly into cash should the need arise.

The money market experts that manage this complex flow of funds must be well educated in the complicated world of finance. They must be able to deal with the maintenance of the bank's legal reserves at the Federal Reserve Bank. They must know the New York money market where a large part of the high-speed, short-term securities are traded to satisfy a bank's immediate money needs. They must understand the complex set of money market forces that make movements in interest rates and bond prices. They must also understand the economic and financial forces that influence the money market.

This small group of experts maintain the billions of bank deposit dollars that are held in securities. These securities and short-term loans are constantly moving to keep the bank solvent. At Bank of America, for example, trading in these short-term claims runs well over $2.5 billion every day. This includes the trading of Federal funds where the transaction is usually for only one day.

A large part of the management involves dealing in U.S. Government securities that are highly liquid and easily bought or sold. Many hundreds of millions of dollars are traded each day over the telephone in U.S. Government securities to help the banks maintain their deposit responsibilities and keep every spare deposit dollar earning a maximum return. Bank of America is a trading participant in all of these markets.

The cashier's department also handles a bank's municipal and government bond holdings. In simple terms, bonds are issued to raise money—they are like IOU's. Whoever issues them agrees to pay back the buyer a certain amount of money within a specified period of time.

Bonds, for example, are sold by states or any of their political subdivisions, such as a city, a school district, or a hospital district. In this category fall such bonds as state school-aid bonds; state veterans bonds; city bonds for the general improvement of streets and public buildings. Hospital district bonds, school district bonds, and sanitation district bonds may, of course, include several cities. By buying or *underwriting* these bonds, banks and other institutions provide governments and municipalities the money they need to meet civic costs—and they provide themselves a steady and safe source of income that can be readily converted to cash should the need arise.

Once a bank buys bonds there is no reason they must hold them until maturity. Besides underwriting initial bond issues, banks may deal in a secondary bond market. That is, they can resell bonds to other banks or institutions and buy bonds from them. There is a regular bond market—something like the stock market—to handle these transactions.

The people who work in a bank's bond department require a variety of talents. Those who underwrite new bond issues need a broad financial background—an ability to assess accurately the hundreds of various factors that will make a bond a good buy or a bad one—and knowledge of the stability, soundness, and general characteristics of various governments and municipalities that issue bonds.

Those who are called traders, who buy and sell secondary bonds, must be well versed in the intricacies of the market, be able to work rapidly and sometimes under great pressure, and must be aware of the minute-to-minute fluctuations as well as the broad trends of bond prices and values.

Since all buying and selling is done by word of mouth, accuracy in keeping records is vital. In this fast-paced work, verbal contracts are binding. The alertness and skill demanded of the traders in the course of an ordinary day's work is reflected in the card one of our bond department employees used to keep on his desk. It read: "May I have the courage to buy the one that can be sold and the wisdom to pass the one that cannot be sold and the sense to know the difference between the two."

Maintenance of the bank's accounting system also utilizes the talents and training of a wide variety of specialists, of particular interest to those inclined toward mathematical or analytical assignments. In a large bank with an extensive branch system, such as Bank of America, obviously the consolidation, analysis, and reporting of statement and earnings figures involve many complexities and individual responsibilities.

These include accurate preparation of daily, weekly, and other periodic reports to governmental agencies as to the bank's condition. Of equal importance are the reports and interpretative analyses provided to management for the same purpose, as well as developing comparative data concerning current performances and future trends. If you are contemplating a career in this area, a good foundation in taxes, statistical analysis, and monetary economics is essential.

Banking and the Law

When you consider that nearly every routine aspect of banking involves state or Federal laws, rules, or regulations, any small error becomes a very serious matter. So, to minimize the chances for such problems and possible losses, many banks maintain a full-time staff of attorneys to advise management, branch and administrative personnel on the legal aspects of their banking operations.

This does not mean that all problems which arise out of a

banking transaction are routine. Since every business organization uses banking services, the bank lawyer must deal with the problems of every type of business—manufacturing, construction, mining, farming, retail selling, education, professional services, and many others. On occasions, for example, Bank of America is even named a co-defendant in divorce proceedings! This usually happens when one party obtains a court order to prevent the other from withdrawing funds from a joint bank account. In such cases, the bank merely complies with the order until the couple works out its differences.

Suits brought against the bank involving claims of personal injury occurring on bank property are usually referred to the bank's insurance company. But in any other cases where claims or demands are made against the bank, the legal department will handle them. Some suits involve huge sums of money—once Bank of America was sued in a Federal court for $11 million—but suits for such sums are usually found to be based more on imagination than fact. The plaintiff in this particular case claimed that business associates were to have deposited money to his account, but when he tried to withdraw the funds to pick up the option on an invention, the bank would not give him the money. Our legal department prepared for the hearing but when the papers were served ordering the man to appear in court, he was in jail on another charge. Needless to say, the case was dropped.

In another case, a customer complained that the bank had allowed someone to open his safe deposit box and some valuable securities had been removed. No action was taken because the person who had been given access to the box was the customer's court-appointed guardian.

Bank lawyers also handle suits to collect money borrowed from the bank when customers prove to be less anxious to repay than they were to borrow. Most people are honest, but occasionally, someone attempts to defraud the bank. In such cases, the bank's legal department leaves no stone unturned in pursuing the culprit. This is necessary not only to prevent losses but, also, to let the public know that banks do not tolerate dishonesty.

Another large area of a legal department's work extends beyond the bank itself and goes into the field of legislation. Our legal department follows proposed state and Federal legislation, looking for any bills that might be of interest to the bank. After the bills have been evaluated by the affected departments, we work with legislative representatives or other interested organizations either in support of or opposition to the bills.

But the most important function of a bank's legal trouble shooters is the one first mentioned—to advise management, branches, and departments. They are always ready and eager to study and interpret the law on all proposed policies, agreements, and transactions to prevent possible controversy before it has a chance to start.

Who Watches the Wealth?

The person who combines an intense interest in the well being of others with an understanding of the principles of sound financial planning can often make a place for himself in a bank's trust department. Trust officers take care of other people's money and assets—through investment advisory services, complete trust management, and estate administration.

People invest their money for a variety of reasons: some to supplement current income, others to provide funds for some future need such as college or retirement. In many cases the management of such investments requires more time than a business or professional person has or more experience than, say, an elderly widow might possess. These are some of the people to whom a bank's trust department offers assistance.

When customers approach a trust officer, the first job usually is to make a preliminary review of their holdings. These may include too many speculative items, purchased solely on long-shot gambles and without knowledge of realistic prospects. Or there may be too many stocks purchased because of a currently attractive yield without knowledge of the company's prospects for continuing such a yield. Also, there may be a lack of sufficient representation in growth industries most likely to benefit from industrial expansion. Or too large a proportion of the fund may be invested in fixed-income securities selling above their call price. Whatever the strengths and deficiencies of any particular set of assets, the trust officer will point them out to the customer and make constructive suggestions.

But the job does not end here. Customers may turn their holdings over to the bank for safekeeping and periodic review. The Trust Department maintains a continuous study of business conditions in general, financial trends, specific industries, individual corporations, and factors affecting real estate. By study and research, a high degree of competence is maintained by trust officers on all forms of security investments—common stocks, corporate bonds, municipal bonds, and government bonds. Changes in holdings will be recommended whenever the situation warrants. Where the bank is entrusted with complete investment responsibility, the necessary action will be taken at once. In agency accounts, changes will not actually be accomplished until the customer approves.

For the customer with securities, the trust officer will collect coupons, dividends, and principal funds when due and remit them directly or credit them to the customer's bank account. Notices of stockholder's meetings or impending reorganizations are forwarded to the customer, temporary bonds are exchanged for permanent ones on issue, ownership certificates are executed, as necessary, attention of customers is directed to options for conversion or exchange of securities, and periodic statements of all transactions are prepared by computer with special attention directed to tax data. The customer with real estate receives the same type of time-saving service: collecting rents, supervising repairs, leasing properties, paying taxes and utilities, making insurance and loan payments, checking real estate valuation for tax assessments, remitting net income in accordance with the customer's instructions, and sending out periodic statements of all transactions.

The trust officer assumes even broader responsibilities when a customer appoints the bank trustee or executor of an estate. A trust is an expression of confidence, in writing, under which all or part of a customer's assets are transferred to the bank for a defined purpose. A testamentary trust is established under the terms of a customer's will and does not take effect until his or her death. In either case, the bank specifically the trust officer, undertakes the same sort of duties as those carried out in performing investment management service.

Lest the trust officer's job begin to sound a bit dull or routine, let me assure you, it is not. People hold their wealth in many forms. Trust department employees in an institution the size of Bank of America may find themselves managing a stable full of race horses one day and a coast-to-coast chain of restaurants the next. These are jobs that demand versatility, sound judgment, an ability to communicate, and perhaps most important, the knack for developing the confidence, friendship, and respect of others.

What Makes a Bank Tick?

As far as most people are concerned, the automobile is a means of moving from one point to another. But it will not do the job unless properly maintained and cared for. It needs gas and oil occasionally, new parts must be provided when old ones wear out or become obsolete, tires must be checked regularly and overall performance must be observed and evaluated on a continuous basis.

Now in banking you have a somewhat similar situation. Most of a bank's business consists of moving money and wealth from one area to another, from idle uses into productive uses. To do so effectively requires that the machinery of banking be in top running condition. And that machinery includes both equipment and procedures. Responsibility for providing, maintaining, and improving bank machinery falls within the area called "operations." This broad field includes literally hundreds of different types of jobs—far too many to cover here. But we might just take a look at a few of them to give you an idea of the scope involved.

The simple act of spending money holds a special, almost unique fascination for six out of every ten persons. But the enormous task of anticipating a large bank's material needs—and purchasing sufficient quantities of different basic supplies required to keep the bank's activities activated—differs somewhat from a Saturday visit to the local supermarket. It is a task that rests on the shoulders of the purchasing department, an important member of the overall operations team.

Buying for a Bank of America-sized organization means

supplying more than 50,782 staff members with stationery, pencils, pens, rubber bands, paper clips, cash boxes, desks, typewriters, rubber stamps, chairs, safe deposit boxes, ink pads, file cabinets, adding machine tape, deposit pass books, special forms, and all the rest of banking's special "tools of the trade." Purchasing is a highly specialized field, in which a number of factors are taken into consideration. Of these, three can be called "basic factors." They are quality, delivery, and price.

Naturally, buyers are concerned with obtaining, on each and every purchase, the most advantageous price available. For this reason, they purchase only on a "bid" basis, which means that competitive prices are solicited from a number of vendors. Ordinarily, vendors are allowed seven working days to complete and return their written bids, although on extremely large orders or specially fabricated items, a longer period is sometimes allowed. After bids have been returned and recorded, it would indeed be an easy matter to simply pick the lowest price and issue a purchase order or contract, except that this would be exceedingly poor purchasing technique. Indeed, price is a most important factor, but as mentioned earlier, it is only one of the three basic considerations which must be weighed in selecting the ultimate supplier.

At Bank of America hundreds of separate purchase orders are issued each month, but our buyers go over each bid from each potential supplier with the proverbial fine-toothed comb. And the savings they are able to effect, just in a few years, are of almost heroic proportions. The total savings are even more impressive when you consider the penny-sized savings on individual purchases that go to make it up. For example, one of our buyers recently detected a possible four cents an ounce savings on a certain product widely used in branch work. Doesn't sound like much? Well, the purchasing department ordinarily buys 10,000 ounces at a time. This adds up to a $400 savings on one purchase order, and that $400 savings is based on comparative prices when purchased in large wholesale quantities. Independent purchases by individual branches would have boosted the price an additional $800 or more, so purchasing actually was responsible for the saving of $1200, just on one order of one minor item.

Efficient purchasing functions then are a *must* to all business organizations. The attitude of "I forgot to order some" or "I'll just run out and buy a box" could quickly take the costs of doing business and push them out of sight. Though perhaps not one of the most publicized members of a bank's operations team, the purchasing department is certainly one of the most important.

The advent of automated banking—the use of computers to perform routine accounting and bookkeeping tasks—has brought a revolutionary change in the character of bank operations. Around this change have sprung up a variety of new jobs, all of an operational nature, which at first glance might seem totally unrelated to banking. Communications analysts, senior cycle collectors, premises analysts, conversion supervisors—certainly these do not seem typical banking titles, yet they all have a place in the modern banking industry. Let's take a closer look at one of the more common jobs in a bank's computer operations—that of the computer systems analyst, sometimes referred to as a *programmer* because part of his job involves telling computers what to do.

For example, getting computers to process real estate loans involves, among many other things, giving detailed instructions on how to calculate interest. Each step requires a separate set of instructions. Each variable, and each possible error point in each step of each process must be foreseen. Then instructions to handle any contingency must be developed into the "program" or "system." Finally, these are written in the particular language of the computers being used. All in all, Bank of America programmers used some three hundred and fifty instruction steps in setting up our computers to calculate just the interest on various types of real estate loans. The entire real estate loan accounting task involves a program containing forty thousand separate instructions which required eleven man years of research and development. And after each basic project has been implemented, programmers are kept busy with modifications to meet new regulations or changes in policy, as well as refinements to incorporate new techniques and procedures. Bank of America now has hundreds of different electronic data processing programs requiring millions of separate instructions—and there are still many more to come. With banks across the nation making similar strides in this important field, you may rest assured that computer systems analysts and their associates will find a strong demand for their talents in financial institutions.

But it takes more than wishful thinking to become a good systems analyst. You must be able to understand the entire scope of any proposed application, from the policy level to detailed operational problems at branches, from the overall aims of management to the legal rules, regulations, and restrictions affecting your subject. You must have an intimate understanding of all the bank's electronic equipment, and must be able to foresee all possible problems and their solutions, as solvable by the equipment available. You must be outgoing enough to interview effectively various bank employees to learn of problems in their areas, and yet introverted enough to return to your office and develop solutions in careful and minute detail.

Because of their nature and their significance to the bank's operations, systems projects characteristically have ambitious target dates. Thus, on occasion, the analysts must be able to devote long hours to a project, particularly when the target date approaches and time becomes a critical factor. They may work both early and late, often including weekends, and then receive a 3:00 A.M. call at home if one of the programs hits a snag on the twenty-four-hour electronic processing equipment. Like military leaders, they must know logistics, understanding the total objectives while directing individual units. Their powers of communication must be varied. Not only do they communicate in trilingual machine language, but also with equipment manufacturers in their own highly specialized jargon, and with lay people in common, everyday English as they write proposals for possible applications, and instruction manuals for completed ones.

Obviously, a high intelligence is required—an educated intelligence, since the systems analyst must continuously learn and keep abreast of the latest technical advances. Yet even more is necessary. The prospective analyst must have an aptitude for systems work. Some people are tone deaf. Some have perfect pitch. The tone deaf person can never be a musician, no matter how intelligent. The same is true in systems analysis.

Because electronics is a complex and rapidly changing field, operations specialists spend much of their time planning for the future. This planning takes two forms: (1) devising new programs and determining new equipment needs that apply to the bank's internal operations, and; (2) devising new data processing services that can be sold to bank customers. Originally, electronic equipment was installed for bank bookkeeping, accounting, and reporting; however, as the demand for new financial accounting services to business and industry increased, special computer applications were developed to satisfy these needs and to once again expand the full financial service concept of progressive banking. For example, a firm can now have its entire payroll prepared and processed by a bank. Companies and stores can "hire" a bank to handle their billing and accounting. These and a variety of other business services are continually being developed and offer bankers new opportunities to specialize.

This by no means represents the full measure of duties included in bank operations. Supervising staff, assigning duties, reviewing performance, maintaining premises, assuring that proper security, accounting, and reporting procedures are carried out—responsibility for these and a thousand other day-to-day factors fall to the people who compose a bank's operational force.

The Cloak and Dagger Set

Just in case you don't think banks have a little of everything, take a look at the loss investigation section of Bank of America's controllers department.

A controllers department is the "watchdog" of the banking business. It assumes responsibility in matters pertaining to budget and cost and the inspection of bank and branch records. This involves measuring the cost of various bank services and functions against their profitability, determining that records are kept in a uniform and legal manner, and recommending structural and procedural improvements. The job is a complex one involving special training in accounting and finance. Let's focus on the loss investigation section not because it is the most important or the biggest, but for the outsider looking in, it seems a rather unusual activity for a banker to be involved in. Nothing could be further from the truth.

The danger of loss is ever-present in a profession whose major commodity is service and whose main instrument of service is money—money in its many and various forms. Losses cover a multitude of errors, omissions, and oversights. Everything from counterfeit currency to tellers' cash shortages falls into the category. Forged or fictitious checks, payments made against uncollected funds, misplaced or overlooked stop payment orders, overpayments, forged U.S. savings bonds or postal money orders, lost or stolen travelers cheques or cashier's checks, overdrafts—these and more are all too frequent operating losses that make heavy inroads on bank profits.

But this profit erosion would be substantially higher were it not for our bank's own squad of special agents who wage constant war against operating losses. These "private eyes" track down forgers, phony check artists, and other fraud operators, assist in their arrest, initiate either civil or criminal action against offenders, and help victimized branches to recover losses.

Thanks to TV's fascination with the subject, the role of the prosecutor is a well known part of the field of law enforcement. Equally dramatized, but less well understood, is the role of the special agent who, in this case, is concerned not only with the detection and apprehension of the fraudulent operator, but also with obtaining, preserving, and reporting facts which provide the basis for establishing admissible evidence for presentation by prosecutors. In these activities, a special agent becomes almost an "assistant to the prosecutor."

Although some three-quarters of all loss cases handled by loss investigations are criminal in nature, our special agents sign complaints to initiate criminal action only after establishing proof. When intent cannot be proved, our agents concentrate on recovery or restitution, since lack of proof in the form of admissible evidence can lead to suit for false arrest. This is but one of the myriad technicalities of the criminal code, commercial law, and rules of admissible evidence that make it necessary for agents to be well informed and to stay on their toes. It is these qualified experts who must determine the course to pursue, and the final action to be taken in each case. During investigation, special agents work not only with agents and investigators of other banks and businesses, but also with Federal and state district attorney's offices, local police and sheriff's offices, the FBI and the U.S. Treasury Department.

Agents help to track down offenders, and initiate legal action where necessary. They also appear in court to identify defendants, act as or arrange for prosecution witnesses, and present evidence. Scarcely a week goes by when three of four of our special agents are not appearing in court. Obviously in addition to having a solid banking background, the agents must possess a working knowledge of the law and the techniques of criminal investigation. With patience and levelheaded reasoning, they can help a bank recover much of what is lost to fraudulent operators—and prevent those same operators from striking again.

Analyzing Economic Trends

We live in an age and economy characterized by complexity and uncertainty. Since bankers must make decisions in this complex and uncertain economy, they often call upon trained specialists—economists—to assist them in gathering and interpreting information about economic developments.

The work they do helps bankers to determine the wisdom and soundness of present practices. It aids them in planning for future expansions, investments, cutbacks, or major policy changes.

For this reason, many banks and businesses have their own economics departments, staffed by professional economists. At Bank of America, for example, our economics department prepares, for internal use, reports which review current conditions in the state of California and the United States. By studying so-called economic indicators such as unemployment, retail sales, housing, and many others, these reports demonstrate the differences between one area and another and provide the bank's management with an important decision-making tool.

Since California is a state rich in agricultural interests, a number of our economists devote a good deal of time to tracing current trends and economic developments in this area. By the same token, because Bank of America has extensive international holdings, some of our economists concentrate on studying foreign markets and economic conditions.

The department also prepares an annual business forecast, assists in reviewing the bank's past performance, develops periodic studies of specific California areas and of the state as a whole and carries on extensive research projects in problem areas of particular concern to the banking industry.

Becoming an economist requires a high degree of professional training—often a doctor's degree and usually at least a master's degree in economics. With growing emphasis being placed upon statistical analysis, intensive training in mathematics and statistics is also advisable. Beyond this, facility in writing and public speaking will also be helpful to the economist who desires to play an important role in the business world—to communicate effectively that which has been learned through research.

Salesmen and Diplomats

The guiding principle of any commercial bank is to serve well the financial needs of others. Putting this principle into practice, however, requires consideration of two important corollaries. First, to "serve well," the bank must maintain the friendship and good will of its customers. Second, it must endeavor to seek out and develop new customers who can benefit from bank services.

In a large institution, special departments may be created to assist in performing these corollary functions. At Bank of America, for example, the people in our business relationships department are specifically assigned to help branches develop new deposits, convert prospects into customers, and to assist these customers in getting total banking service. Moreover, we have specific divisions within the department to deal with specific groups of customers.

Our national division is responsible for the development of bank and major corporate business throughout the country. We have representatives traveling the entire United States and Eastern Canada, calling on financial vice presidents, corporation treasurers, and banks where we have correspondent relationships. In-state, our national division officers do the same thing among the larger firms whose headquarters are in California. Each call is made for the purpose of obtaining more new business and assuring that we are doing everything possible to maintain a strong and favorable relationship with our customers. Moreover, whenever we hear of out-of-state firms exploring new locations in California, contemplating mergers, sales or expansions of business, or even developing new products here, our national division is called into action immediately. Performing a similar function but dealing with a different group of customers is our category division which helps branches obtain public deposits from state, city, and county officials, and all types of political subdivisions.

Our area and community development divisions have still another group of customers as their target. To understand fully the service these divisions provide, a little background may be helpful. The challenges of community development have been with us for a good many years. More than a century ago someone described a California mining town as "frame shanties pitched together as if by accident; tents of canvas, of blankets, of brush, of potato sacks and old shirts, with empty whiskey barrels for chimneys; piles of goods and rubbish on craggy points, in the hollows, on the rocks, in the mud, on the snow, everywhere scattered in pellmell confusion."

It is probably safe to say this community was somewhat in need of at least a modest self-improvement program. But in those days the challenge was less pressing. When conditions became unbearably deplorable, inhabitants could simply pack up and move on to greener or, as in many cases then, more golden pastures. Today this opportunity does not so readily present itself. Between 1975 and 1985, the population of California is expected to increase from 21,206,000 to 24,-363,000. Of this figure approximately one million, or more than 8,000 per month, will be new residents who will have moved here from other states or countries. These 100,000 new Californians per year will expect to be housed, fed and employed or educated if they are too young to enter the employment market. Unless Californians are prepared to make a lemming-like march into the Pacific Ocean, they must learn to solve these community and area development challenges by management rather than migration.

In recent years many communities have come to this realization and the consequent demand for information and guidance has been so great that a systematic body of knowledge centered around community development has evolved. No one is in a better position than the banker to observe what has been done, what new experiments are being tried, and in a broad sense, how successful various approaches to community development might be. For this reason Bank of America, along with other banks in the country, has established area and community development divisions. Staff members in these activities act strictly in an advisory capacity. They consult with and provide material to communities interested in downtown redevelopment; urban renewal projects; industrial development; making better use of resources; solving water, school, park, or slum problems; and the array of other problems connected with community or area development. The efforts of these divisions do not of course, always mean the immediate gain of new business for the bank; but they invariably serve to strengthen the ties between the bank and the communities it serves.

So far we have seen only those divisions of the business

relationships department which deal with specific customer groups—groups like the corporation, the local government, and the community. For the most part, these divisions are staffed by seasoned bankers with special knowledge of their customers' problems. They are outgoing individuals with a knack for making new friends easily and they are excellent salesmen—able to relate the needs of a complex organization to the services a bank offers. But what about individual customers—those who have $100 saving accounts and checking accounts with average balances of $50? They also are important; their good will is as vital to the bank as that of large corporate customers. They must be kept informed about new bank services; their complaints must be heard and answered; and the bank must be constantly on the alert for new ways to increase its stature in their eyes.

In large measure, getting through to these people is a problem in communication, but a big bank has so many individual customers, that reaching each one in person on a regular basis is virtually impossible. Only by using radio, television, newspapers, magazines, special publications and by having bank officers speak before large groups can an institution keep open a continuing line of communication with the general public. This is where a bank's advertising and public relations departments come into the picture.

While advertising officers may depend upon a professional agency to actually write and produce advertisements, they are responsible for determining what particular services and events should be advertised, deciding where the ads should be placed, coordinating with various other departments in the bank, and planning and supervising overall campaigns.

Since a good advertising program has to be placed on firm ground, members of Bank of America's department spend a great deal of time travelling. "We like to talk to branch managers and officers," says one of our advertising officers, "so we can understand their problems and interpret their needs through advertising. It's part of our philosophy that getting out and contacting people directly is the best way to make our program both vital and realistic."

Reflecting this approach one series of testimonial ads was used in which prominent California farmers and ranchers state in simple, straightforward language how Bank of America services had helped them to operate successfully. The ads, appeared in farm publications and farm sections of newspapers in agricultural areas and gained personal appeal from being accompanied by an artist's sketch of the farmer.

Whenever a specific department is involved in a promotional campaign, an advertising officer works in close cooperation to develop a plan. If, for example, a brochure on the trust department is planned, two representatives of the advertising department and a trust officer will get together to thresh out and analyze possible ideas for a presentation of maximum effectiveness. When the idea and angle of presentation are finally selected, the agency prepares a rough layout and submits it to the advertising and trust officers for approval. Before the brochure even begins to take final form, it has run the full gamut of criticism from a number of different experts. The finished product has eye appeal, clarity, and sincerity of message, and a certain bright originality that gives it the stamp of distinctive advertising.

The advertising department is also called upon from time to time to purchase premium gifts—pens, key chains, cigarette lighters, and a variety of other small useful items. These are then imprinted with an advertising message, usually in the form of a slogan and presented to the public on various special occasions. "Signing" constitutes still another area of advertising responsibility. Each Bank of America branch is equipped with one or more signs which identify the facility and to the maximum extent possible, enhance its appearance. Advertising officers visit future branch sites and take along a camera and blueprint, or plot plan. From the general physical layout they judge the angle from which the signs will have the greatest visibility and effectiveness. They take particular note of the architectural materials that predominate in the vicinity and check to see whether or not a sign should be illuminated. If, for example, the shopping area surrounding the branch has a rustic decor, the sign will be constructed of suitable materials.

Thus, through one medium of communication or another, a bank's advertising department helps to keep the institution's name before the public eye. At Bank of America, the advertising staff prepares well over 2,000 ads annually. A performance on such a large scale demands the closest kind of teamwork with other bank departments and among advertising staff members, not to mention an immense amount of creative energy.

A public relations department is equally concerned with communications but in a somewhat different way than the advertising department. Advertisements are for the most part selling messages, designed to persuade as well as inform. The space they occupy in a newspaper or magazine and the time they take up on radio or television is *paid* for. Publicity, on the other hand, is *news*. It is carried by communications media for its own interest value to the general public.

For example, when Bank of America opens a new branch, when we enter a new field of banking service such as leasing, or when one of our senior officers makes a speech on new developments in bank automation—this is news. And as such, it is the concern of our public relations department. The publicity section of the department may in fact operate much as a newspaper does. It is composed of writers who, like newspaper reporters, cover specific "beats" in the bank. Their job is to uncover news stories, write them, and release them to local and national news media that might be interested. They are also responsible for maintaining regular and friendly relationships with members of the press both through frequent contact and by providing background information about the bank when asked to.

The editorial services section of the public relations department gives bank speakers assistance in preparing talks and arranging speaking engagements. This section also helps prepare various publications from time to time, such as the annual report to stockholders. Still another section of the department initiates and administers various public service programs designed to improve bank relationships with the people we serve. For example, this section handles Bank of America's Achievement Awards Program, which provides California high school students with $214,000 in scholarships each year.

In both advertising and public relations the accent is heavily upon the creative skills—artistic and verbal talents are a must. Obviously, newspaper background is valuable in publicity work, but overall, the general ability to translate complex financial concepts into simple understandable terms is the prime requisite for success in public relations and advertising work.

There is one more division in this broad field of business relationships which deserves our attention. In a sense it represents the "moment of truth." We never know how well we are communicating with our customers unless the results of our efforts are measured in some scientific way. This task falls to the marketing research division.

Through surveys and interviews of our customers, the people in marketing research can determine the success of current programs. If there are any serious areas of customer dissatisfaction or disappointment, our marketing experts will expose them. If we are contemplating the introduction of a new service, marketing research can gauge in advance what the public reaction will be. In short, this division helps us to evaluate the overall success of our business relationships activities and gives us a foundation for planning new programs. Moreover, it performs a vital task in developing premises location surveys. Largely on the basis of these surveys, the bank decides when and where to open a new branch or relocate an old one. A good knowledge of people, a quick and inquiring mind, and a professional acquaintance with modern marketing techniques are the minimum requirements for success in this important field.

Looking after Human Resources

We have mentioned customers and the importance of developing and retaining their good will. There is another group of people who are equally important—a bank's own employees. They constitute an institution's most valuable resource and require close attention and constant cultivation. Large banks, like all good-sized corporations, maintain a staff to hire, train, review the progress of, and promote employees. At Bank of America, these are functions of bankwide Personnel Administration.

Employee relations officers are responsible for seeing that

personnel practices conform to company policy and government regulation. Each employee has an individual file that includes employment information, periodic performance reviews and other pertinent information. Staff members set up job specifications, determine salary levels, keep a close check on personnel morale, administer employee benefit plans, and assume responsibility for informing employees of bank-wide developments that might be of general interest. Aside from a general banking background, training in professional personnel management techniques and psychology will help you launch a successful career in this field.

As for the training officer, a true story best illustrates the varied talents needed in order to do this job well. It was back in 1958 when the development of efficient and economical computers encouraged us to convert from a manual to an electronic system of bookkeeping. The conversion was statewide, scheduled to take place over a short period of time, and its ramifications extended to nearly every segment of our operational structure. As you may well imagine, the work load thrust upon our training and development staff was colossal.

First came the task of selling the idea of letting computers take over the drudgery of bookkeeping. Then it was necessary to transmit the technical details to people at every job level in our branches. Managers were trained in those changes pertinent to their responsibilities, operations officers needed a different package, tellers still another, and so on—thus the amount and variety of communication required was tremendous. And, at the same time, it was necessary to counsel and relate our plans for retraining and allocating new—and frequently higher level—assignments to those staff members whose positions would be affected by the conversion.

Still more remained to be done. Computers then were new enough so that trained computer systems personnel were in short supply. For this reason, our training officers had to launch a program designed to turn some young bankers into automation specialists. This was no easy assignment. Yet it was accomplished. And to this day, a large number of the employees—indeed many of the experts—in our systems and equipment division are individuals who were once preautomation bankers.

Thus you can see we expect a good deal of our trainers at Bank of America. They must be efficiency experts of a sort —able to impart maximum amounts of information with optimum effectiveness in minimum time and at minimum cost. They must be good bankers, with more than a glancing familiarity with lending techniques, operational procedures, and public relations policy. They must be skilled teachers, alert to the new educational techniques and aware of their strengths and deficiencies. Should the need arise for a training pamphlet or manual, a sound slide film, or motion picture, the trainer must rise to the occasion and become writer, artist, and movie director.

For those who show an early interest in this field, the future looks bright. Technology and automation are developing today with greater rapidity and complexity than ever before. New positions with new skill requirements are being created and old roles are being redefined. The trainer plays a major role in helping to make these transitions smoothly and effectively.

These, then, are some of the people and some of the talents necessary in the day-to-day operation of a large modern bank. The various classifications I have given are arbitrary and may well vary from bank to bank. In some cases, one department may combine five or six of the responsibilities I have assigned to separate departments. As a general rule, however, you will find that larger banks manifest a greater number of specialized activities than smaller banks. And, of course, the most interesting point to keep in mind is that the banking profession is almost a world in itself, offering attractive career opportunities to people of almost every bent. This variety makes banks fascinating places in which to work—for while pursuing your own particular line of endeavor, you remain close to current developments in a wide range of other important and interesting areas.

CHAPTER IV

Meanwhile, Back at the Branch

The last time I visited in Markleeville, there were eighty-five people living in this little town perched high on the slopes of California's Sierra Nevada mountains. Markleeville had no churches, no movie theatres, no undertakers. There was not even a doctor living there.

But Markleeville does have a bank—a community office of Bank of America. It occupies two rooms in the local motel and serves the financial needs of nearby residents and the occasional hunter or fisherman who is just "passing through." It is the smallest of Bank of America's more than 1,000 branch facilities throughout California. And clearly, the range of jobs available in one of these small to medium-sized branches—the procedures which compose a normal day's business—differ greatly from those outlined in the previous chapter. A well-rounded understanding of banking careers requires that we consider conditions in a small institution as well as a large one, so let's have a closer look at a typical small bank.

The Best of Both

The general distinctions between working in a small and large bank were examined earlier but they bear more detailed repeating here:

1. A large bank offers the employee a wide range of specialized activities, some having only a casual connection with finance and banking. The activities of a small bank are divided into two broad categories: credit services and operations. There are only two or three types of jobs available in each of these categories, and generalized rather than specialized abilities are called for.
2. Young people just beginning their careers are apt to have less competition at their own age level in a small bank than in a large one. For this reason, it is easier to move into a position of authority more rapidly. Also, the chances of exerting a degree of personal influence over the organization—an opportunity to play a fundamental role in setting policy and making crucial decisions—will be greater than in a large institution.
3. If you are aiming for a large bank, you may as well reconcile yourself to living in one of our urban financial centers: New York, Chicago, San Francisco, Los Angeles, and so on. Few major corporations establish headquarters in the countryside. Small banks, on the other hand, present a broad choice of living areas. You can reside in the mountains, or on the desert, by the seaside, or on the plains—communities in all these types of areas usually have a local bank. It follows that the small bank in a small town offers you greater opportunities for establishing a measure of civic promi-

nence and prestige. In a large city you will likely be but one of many anonymous people contributing to the public good.

4. Many of the jobs in a large bank involve very little direct customer contact. In nearly every job a small bank offers, you will come into frequent and continuous contact with your customers.
5. It is difficult to generalize about salaries, but in most cases the bigger the bank, the better the pay. There are two principal reasons for this. Wages and costs of living seem to run higher in large urban areas and to compete with other large institutions for employees, big banks must pay competitive prices. As we have seen, big banks also demand more specialized abilities—and in cases where those abilities have been developed through professional training and education, they can command a higher than average salary. For the most part, a small bank neither needs nor can afford such high-priced talent.

I have stated that a branch banking system can provide the best of the benefits found in both large and small banks. Let me elaborate. Consider three banks, X, Y, and Z. X is in a large metropolitan city with a population over one million and a diverse economy including shipping interests; agricultural, canning, and packing activities; service-based firms; and light and heavy industry. Y is in a medium-sized industrial community composed mostly of middle-class families who work in the local electronics and manufacturing firms. Z is in a tiny farm community whose income depends almost entirely on the production of wheat and other grains.

Bankers at Z will receive the typical advantages and disadvantages any small town bank has to offer. In addition they will probably become quite proficient in the field of crop, livestock, and commodity loans and in financing farm machinery. Bankers at Y will probably earn about the same salary, and their opportunities will be much the same—however, their knowledge in the area of industrial and consumer financing will become fairly specialized as this is where much of his business will be. Finally, bankers at X will have open to them the variety of pursuits available in a large bank. They can specialize in industrial, consumer, agricultural financing, or a host of other fields besides.

Now, if X, Y, and Z are each unit banks, it is unlikely that the employees of one will have much contact with those of another. Of course, bankers in Z could quit their jobs and go to work in bank Y. Later they could quit their jobs at Y and go to X. In this way they would receive the different benefits that each town and bank had to offer. But suppose banks Y and Z are branches of a large headquarters bank, X. A young banker might begin a career in Z, be moved to Y when all that Z had to offer had been learned and eventually end up at X, as a specialist and adviser in some particular field. In this way, these bankers could develop the very broadest sort of banking experience, working in many sizes and types of towns, and being exposed to a variety of different fields. Eventually, they wind up as experts, gaining more pay more responsibility, and more authority at each step in the process. And all this happens without having to quit one organization and join another.

The advantages of remaining with the same organization are obvious. You learn its general policies and practices; and the institution in turn comes to know your particular strengths and weaknesses and arranges your career program and salary schedule accordingly. Each time you change employers, this "get acquainted" process must begin all over again. Each year you spend with the same organization strengthens its loyalty to you and hence, your job security. Also, as you build seniority, you participate more fully in employee benefit plans. You play more important and decision-making roles and have an edge on other employees who are of approximately equal age and ability but have been with the company a shorter time. This is not to say a person should never switch jobs. There are times when it is definitely advantageous to do so. But you must weigh carefully the opportunities offered by a new employer against those advantages already gained by remaining with your present employer.

As I describe the work done and the jobs available in a branch bank, here is the point to keep in mind: the same sort of description applies to a small unit bank with two important exceptions: (1) the transition from small bank experience to large bank experience is apt to be made more smoothly in a branch system than in a unit system, and (2) the branch bank may be able to offer customers a wider array of services due to the large resources and expert knowledge available in its administrative headquarters.

Who's in Charge Here?

The key person in a branch bank is the *manager*. The duties are diverse, the responsibilities broad, and the authority great. Perhaps the first responsibility is to the financial needs of the branch's customers. It is up to the manager to see that customers are well acquainted with services offered by the bank—that those services are made available to those who need and qualify for them—and that the branch performs those services in strict accordance with bank policies and practices and with a high degree of courtesy and personal attention. While the manager must be familiar with the entire range of bank services (there may be as many as eighty), it is not necessary to have a detailed working knowledge of each. Lending services constitute by far the most important group and branch managers must be well versed in three major loan classifications:

1. *Commercial Loans:* Loans made to individuals, business firms, and other organizations for the purpose of assisting production, carrying inventory, meeting seasonal needs for working capital, and other requirements.
2. *Real Estate Loans:* Loans for buying or building homes, apartment houses, stores, and other types of property.
3. *Consumer Loans:* Loans usually made to individuals or families for the purchase of household furnishings, appliances, home improvements, automobiles, and other consumer goods and services.

In these three classifications, the manager will often be the final authority for either granting or refusing a loan. The better acquainted with each classification, the better assured the manager will be that customers get the services needed. As we saw in the previous chapter, there are many subcategories within these three broad loan classifications, but the manager need not be highly specialized in each. There are also many other classifications of bank services: deposit services, business services, trust services, municipal finance services, and general customer services to name a few. But if the branch manager has at least a nodding acquaintance with each, the customers will receive first-rate service. How? By calling on the bank's administrative headquarters. Let's see an example of how branch-administration cooperation works.

The setting is a small but prosperous California community largely dominated by a family enterprise which controls much of the industry in the area. The firm has strong and long-standing ties with the local community bank, and family members keep their accounts both with the local bank and with various other financial institutions. When a new branch bank is established in the community, the manager quickly ascertains that community acceptance of the branch depends upon the ability of officers and staff to do business with the town's major enterprise. Accordingly, the manager contacts a high ranking officer of the firm with whose help is drawn up a list of the organization's financial needs.

Next, the manager writes the administrative headquarters, enclosing the list and resulting recommendations, which are forwarded to experts in industrial finance. They find the firm to be sound and prosperous, and the branch manager is so informed. The company then is informed that a certain amount of credit is available at the local branch. The firm immediately makes use of it.

The branch manager simultaneously contacts officers in the headquarters trust department, who prepare a trust package consisting of pension and profit-sharing plans for the firm's employees as well as trust and investment services for members of the owning family. The package is presented by a trust officer and the branch manager and is ultimately accepted.

The headquarter's installment loan experts also cooperate with the manager in preparing an employee loan and deposit service package, which the manager then presents to the firm. Within three months after the manager first made contact with the firm, the employee loan and deposit plan has been accepted and put into effect; loans granted total slightly over $200,000; total deposits of the company and family members total $111,000; and trust department representatives are working out an estate planning program for the family. By taking full advantage of the administration facilities available, this alert and aggressive branch manager gained a profitable new customer and gave the branch a strong competitive position in the community.

Naturally, in providing most services, the manager will handle the entire transaction in the branch. When highly specialized knowledge or unusually large amounts of money are involved, the manager need only pick up the phone and call upon administration for assistance. But in either case, it is the manager who makes initial and continued contact with the customer—it is the manager who sells the bank's services and who must assure that quality of the service remains satisfactory as long as the customer uses it. This means that a good portion of each day will be spent out of the branch, calling on old customers and seeking out new ones.

If the branch manager's first responsibility is to customers, the second is to the community in which he or she works. I know of no better way to express this fact than the manner in which it was set forth by one of Bank of America's branch managers in a speech recently delivered to the local Rotary Club. Here are some selected portions of that talk:

"To some firms, this [responsibility toward the community] is still considered one of the 'niceties' of business. Actually, it is one of the 'necessities.' Bankers nowadays must be well aware of their responsibility toward the communities that they 'live' in. They must recognize that there are two ways in which a banker can fulfill community responsibilities. The first of these is by utilizing the resources of the bank in the best way possible and the second is through the role of an individual citizen with a financial background.

"From the moment when it first opens its door, the bank assumes a responsibility for assisting in the developing of its community. For example, it is responsible not only for financing the construction and operation of business firms, but also for helping to transform new and undeveloped land into attractive residential sections with pleasant, well-kept homes.

"It is the bank's duty to assist purchasers in acquiring goods and services that make possible a better life. And finally, the bank must be willing to assist in the development of those civil projects that mean so much to the well-being of the community as a whole—schools, parks, highways, and other improvements. In short, the banker must continually weigh and evaluate the entire community's growth and well-being.

"The banker also has community responsibilities as an individual. Many banks actively urge their officers to lend their financial know-how to community projects when they are needed. You will find bankers participating in civic undertakings as officers and directors of civic groups; speaking out in behalf of social and philanthropic organizations; taking part in nonpartisan political activities for the good of the community.

"I could give you a long list of bankers in community affairs and the good works they have accomplished. Actually, the banker's responsibility to the community is the same as any other citizen's. Like them, an honest appraisal of the needs of the community—cultural, civic, religious, economic, educational, governmental must be made. The banker must then choose the area or areas which have particular appeal and in which the bank can help most. And then a program must be developed which will fulfill the needs as seen or participate in a program already underway."

It is clear from these observations that a branch manager never quite gets away from the job. When not actually in the branch, the banker may be participating in some civic activity: speaking at a local service club, helping to raise funds for the Red Cross, or working with the city planning board on a new redevelopment project.

There is still another area of responsibility for our branch manager, and that is toward the employees of the branch. They must be hired, trained, evaluated, promoted, encouraged, and in some cases, dismissed. Though the manager may delegate much of this responsibility to others, the ultimate authority on all matters involving a difference of opinion is inherent in this position. In addition a prime responsibility is for the supervision of the lending officers. These are often younger men or women who will one day themselves become branch managers or administrative experts. For credit experience, they are usually assigned to one of the three main loan categories listed above—commercial, real estate, or consumer—and will deal primarily with customers in these areas. It is the manager's duty to review the transactions handled by these officers; to help them develop sound credit judgment; to assist them in particularly difficult or complex situations; and to observe, evaluate, and then either criticize or praise their performance.

Direct jurisdiction over the branch's other employees may be assigned to the operations officer. This position is, in a very real sense, the manager's right arm, so let's review the duties and responsibilities assigned.

Second in Command

A typical day for the operations officer begins on arrival at the branch at 8:00 A.M. The first task is the opening, review and distribution of all incoming mail. Then new circulars and announcements from administrative headquarters must be read and analyzed so that employees concerned can be informed immediately about new or revised policies. Next the vault's time-lock has released the locking mechanism and the operations officer who has memorized half the combination joins with another person who has memorized the other half and opens the vault. Then important records and the branch supply of coin and currency can be moved to the various places in the branch where they are available for use during the balance of the working day. The first phone call of the day for the operations officer is bad news. One of the branch employees is on the line and will not be in to work because of a severe cold. This means that several staff assignments will have to be shuffled so that all work for the day can be completed on schedule. The changed assignments are discussed with an assistant who supervises tellers, machine operators and several basic clerical functions. Decisions are made, action taken, and now it is time to sit at a desk for a time. Dictation to a secretary so that replies to the morning mail can be dispatched promptly usually has first priority. However, interruptions can occur such as telephone calls from customers requesting special services; bank drafts and general ledger entries requiring signatures for approval; a branch supply order for review and approval and five customers checks that need special handling because of overdrafts; irregular signatures; an incoming wire that must be decoded in order to learn the special instructions concerning transfer of funds for an important customer; assistance for a teller who is handling a transaction involving foreign exchange or acceptance of service of a court order restraining the further use of funds on deposit because of litigation.

By this time, the day is well along, but we only have scratched the surface of a branch operations officer's responsibilities. Though much of the actual work of compiling reports can be delegated and then more carefully reviewed, for accuracy, there are some which require personal attention and efforts. Employee reports and records which are confidential require this kind of personal involvement. The operations officer must be available to discuss work related problems, both business and personal, with staff members who ask for help. This function cannot and should not be delegated. In addition, there are a host of other duties and responsibilities that cannot be delegated such as special requests involving branch personnel, extended vacations, sick leaves, changes in work schedules and possible or projected promotions of staff members.

Many of the duties described are discussed with the branch manager or with concerned officers at administrative headquarters, whose concurrence is necessary in the hiring of a new employee. Induction, orientation and training of new employees and training and development of present staff members are of prime importance and must be included in the routine of the regular daily work load. This means that an operations officer must know, understand and be interested in people. A willingness to help those employees who want to learn, increase and widen their knowledge of banking is one way to judge the operations officers who, in turn are headed toward promotions that will include larger, more interesting and challenging responsibilities.

Although we have been discussing the need for the constant attention of the operations officer to the performance and progress of individual staff members, the position responsibilities include the safeguarding and care of all branch records. A systematic method must be developed to assure that all delegated duties are properly and promptly performed and that accounting procedures as prescribed by bank policy are being followed. If an unaccounted cash difference occurs, then suggestions must be made as to the procedures necessary that will lead to discovery of the error. If necessary, qualified, experienced employees may be assigned to help the employee involved to determine the error that occurred and how it may be corrected. Sometimes the operations officer must authorize charge-off of losses, usually or hopefully minor ones, to loss accounts. On a regular scheduled basis, supervision is given to audit and certification of various accounts. Major certifications include accounts for cash, loans, checking and savings.

The operations officer is joint custodian for valuables, keys and numbered forms, approves charges to accounts for special handling, and receives and replies to credit inquiries and certification of bank balances, reviews checks which have been presented for payment and which cannot be paid because of lack of funds or irregularities in preparation such as lack of date, signature missing, etc., and then approves or disapproves them for payment; checks and approves various accounting entries before processing; reviews reports which have been prepared for the manager, bank administrative headquarters and/or Federal or state agencies such as employee absence records, losses and recoveries, federal government "call" reports, branch budgets twice yearly; arranges vacation schedules; assigns destruction of old records in accordance with official regulations; and may, on special occasions, actively participate in the task involved in locating major cash differences or accounting errors.

All in all, the operations officer's job is to make certain the branch runs smoothly from an internal standpoint. In order to do this, it is essential to have a thorough knowledge of all duties performed in the branch as well as a familiarity with all audits and reports required from each section and department in the branch. Supervisory ability is another important requisite along with that sixth sense for management that is demonstrated by effective organization, coordination and control that results in the continual smooth and orderly flow of work through the office. Basically, an operations officer must like and understand people and be interested in them as people. In large branches, the duties are almost entirely supervisory, while in smaller branches, it is possible only to delegate a few of the audit, training and follow-up duties. Many of the routine reports which in a larger branch would be delegated to a subordinate must be prepared by the operations officer in a smaller facility. Though a great deal of pressure and responsibility attaches itself to this job, it is one which is readily open to young people who are thorough, careful, and intelligent—and who have a flair for hard work.

Putting the Best Foot Forward

Late one Friday evening—it was 5:45 to be exact—a distinguished-looking gentleman walked into the lobby of one of Bank of America's branches. He approached a teller and asked her to open a commercial account for him. The teller examined the customer's impressive credentials and his passbooks from several banks in different states. She noted that the accounts, totaling nearly $15,000, had all been opened the previous month. Everything on the surface seemed authentic and in good order. As the gentleman put his credentials away, he smoothly explained that he would come in the next week to check on the transaction. "I would also like to open my checking account here," he added, "with a $3,000 check drawn on my New York bank." "Fine, sir," said the teller, "but we will have to put a 'hold' on your account until the check has cleared." By this, the teller meant that no checks could be written against the new account until the funds had actually been verified and transferred by the New York bank. In some cases, this may take as long as three days. The gentleman was more than agreeable and politely made his departure.

On Monday, checks he had written to local stores over the weekend began to pour into the branch. The branch manager immediately wired the customer's bank in New York as well as his other bank references. In two of them, the "gentleman" had no funds, and in the other, he had a $10 deposit. The teller, by using her wits and by remembering her training about "holds" on uncollected funds had saved the branch from losing a large sum of money.

The story illustrates two of the principal qualifications any good teller must possess. First, to know the job. In the course of a normal working day, a teller handles scores of different transactions involving scores of different forms and procedures. Whether cashing a check, accepting a savings account deposit, selling travelers cheques, preparing a foreign draft, taking a stop-payment order, or issuing a money order, a teller must know how to perform the task thoroughly and yet rapidly. If a teller handled money awkwardly or forgot to post a loan payment book, the branch would lose customers every day.

But notice also that the teller was invariably polite throughout the story recounted above. And this is the second important quality a teller must exhibit. Tellers know that customers like to conduct their business in an informal, hospitable, warm atmosphere. They never own so much or so little money that they're willing to dispense with friendliness. They thrive on attention and service, whether their business amounts to $5.00 or to $50,000. And when they ask questions, they do not enjoy an answer couched in technical terms. They quite rightly expect their teller to be a polished translator who can simplify banking terminology.

A teller's job is not without excitement and drama. In some cases alertness has been known to help police or government officials. Nearly all tellers, for example, have a working knowledge of how to detect counterfeit bills and coins. Sometimes just a quick comparison of a good bill with a bad one is enough clue for a teller to act. Tellers learn from experience that a bad coin has a greasy feeling and the corrugated outer edge is crooked and indistinct. In a recent case one of our branch tellers recognized the serial numbers on currency taken in the robbery of a Los Angeles bank. She immediately notified the proper officials. Her quick action led to the apprehension of the thief—and a hefty reward to boot.

Nor is a teller's day completely without humor. Not long ago one of our tellers reported that a customer came to her window to exchange two five-dollar bills. She had washed them, she explained, because she couldn't bear to handle dirty money. On this occasion, however, the bills were still wet when she needed some cash, and she scorched them trying to speed up the drying process on her stove. Another teller told how a lady customer came into the branch one afternoon to inquire about the balance in her savings account. The teller checked and reported that the account had not been used in more than six years. To this the lady replied, "Well, I don't get the car very often."

So tellers take humor and drama in stride, realizing both are integral components of their working day. And at the very foundation of the teller's job is a knowledge of people—a knowledge that the satisfied customer is the best customer. Toward this end it is the teller's daily responsibility to put the bank's best foot forward.

Start Small

Managers, loan officers, operations officers, and tellers—these are the people who guide the branch bank through a normal working day. Jobs for stenographers, secretaries, clerks, and business-machine operators can also be found in many branch banks, but they are not as prominent as the positions already mentioned and are largely self-explanatory.

The career-seeker seriously considering banking should not make the mistake of looking askance at small banks. They offer a superb opportunity for broad, general training in all the various facets of banking. Many times the young person who develops competence at every level in a small bank will later on be in a better position for advancement than the young person who starts with a large bank and learns only one particular job. This, of course, is not a hard and fast rule. But in beginning a banking career, you should seek a position that offers broad rather than narrow and specialized experience.

CHAPTER V

A Word to the Women

Several years ago the actions of a cross country confidence man were brought to the attention of Bank of America's travelers cheque department. The young man was going from city to city buying travelers cheques, reporting them missing, and collecting reimbursement from the bank. He would later cash the original cheques.

Successfully eluding police, the thief would pose at various times as an exchange student son of a wealthy South American, as a European ballet dancer, and as a businessman.

Members of our department's investigative division had long suspected that all the fraudulent claims were originating from the same person. But they had been unable to track him down.

Then one day a call came in from Philadelphia. The caller said he was a businessman. He was scheduled to be married the next day in Mexico City, but he had been carrying all his money in the form of travelers cheques and he had lost them. He sought an immediate refund for $1,700.

In talking to him on the phone, one of our investigators recognized the criminal's voice. The Philadelphia police were immediately notified, and our investigator kept the confidence man talking until officers arrived to arrest him.

For our investigative staff, it was just another routine case, successfully brought to a conclusion. For the criminal, the arrest not only meant several years in prison, but also probably came as a severe blow to his ego. The investigator who had outwitted him was not a husky, hard-boiled criminologist, but quite the contrary, a petite, five-foot-two, ash blond woman.

As a matter of fact, for many years, every claims investigator in our travelers cheque department was a woman. Whether it was women's intuition or good detective work (probably a combination of both) this group kept travelers cheque losses to a minimum and recovered hundreds of thousands of dollars by helping to track down forgers, counterfeiters and thieves.

They worked closely with and enjoyed the professional respect of police forces in all continents through Interpol, the FBI, the CID and the U.S. Treasury, as well as local police in hundreds of cities.

Although both men and women now staff the claims activity, for a time women alone performed an important and responsible function for the bank. The success earned here enabled women to move into other banking positions that for too long had been considered only suitable for men.

Ladies in Waiting

The first recorded banking transaction took place 4,000 years ago when a Babylonian sun-priestess loaned two shekels of silver to a citizen of Babylon and decided to "put it in writing." The record was inscribed and baked into a clay tablet. Thus, a woman was the first known lending officer in the history of banking.

But it would be a long wait indeed until women entered the world of finance and banking in any great number. In fact, it was just at the turn of this century that a few courageous women began seeking work outside the home. They applied at offices and factories—as salesladies in stores and teachers in schools. The ranks of working women increased considerably during and after the First World War—they helped to fill the vacancies left by men going into service. During the depression, women once again ventured out of the home and into the business world, this time in order to earn enough to keep their homes together.

For the most part, however, these trends were of a temporary nature. When the pressing need to work had passed, many women returned to their traditional role as wife, mother, and homemaker. It wasn't until the Second World War that women in large numbers became a permanent factor in the labor force. To keep the economy and business running smoothly, they entered the ranks of the employed by the millions. During these years they learned new skills, office procedures, and business responsibilities. New opportunities were opened to women that had never existed before. When the war ended, many of these women had found such a keen interest and stimulation in their jobs that they were reluctant to give them up. A large number of them decided to keep working.

Moreover, there were several post-war developments that encouraged women who had never worked before to enter the job market. More and more families that longed for the "good life" and its material advantages found it necessary to have the women of the household go to work. At the same time, it became social custom that a young girl should seek employment after high school or college graduation.

It's A Woman's World

One of the many wonderful stories about the late Sir Winston Churchill reveals a shrewd and humorous insight on the ability of women. He was asked one day to comment on the prediction that by the year 2,000 women would rule the world. Churchill is reported to have nodded, smiled, and said simply, "They still will, eh?"

Anyone examining the role women play in today's economy would agree that they do indeed already hold a position of power and importance.

The number of women in the working force, for example, is growing by 3.9 percent a year, compared to 1.4 percent for men. In fact, two out of every five workers are women.

The number of women entering professions also is increasing each year. The most recent United States census shows that from 1960 to 1974, the number of women engaged in professional occupations increased 85 percent. This figure is particularly significant in that the number of men engaged in professional occupations during the same period increased 54 percent. Women are entering the professions almost as fast as men.

More women are graduating from our law schools and practicing in all segments of the profession. There is hardly an area where a woman attorney is not practicing today.

There were 1,840 women stockbrokers in 1960, ten times as many as in 1946 but by 1970 the number had increased to 8,880. At all levels of government women can be found in prominent positions. They are being appointed to top assignments in many agencies. They are more active in city, county, state, and federal political elections.

The 1970 Census also shows that in the decade from 1960, women as aeronautical engineers increased 33 percent, as architects by 159 percent, as personnel and labor relations workers by 196 percent, and as public relations and publicity writers by 177 percent.

Female Financiers

Banking offers as dramatic an example as any of women's newfound independence. Before the Second World War, approximately 70 percent of bank employees were men. In recent years this relationship has been reversed and presently 66 percent of bank employees are women. Each year a significantly larger number of women have moved from lower level positions to supervisory and management positions.

It is fitting that women should be so active in today's financial community. American women make most of the family purchases, they own 75 percent of stocks and bonds and 65 percent of the nation's savings accounts. In addition, the number of employed women continues to increase and in 1975 has reached an all time high of 112 million with combined annual salaries of $116 billion. Ten years ago the total annual earnings of women was only $45 billion.

At Bank of America we employ thousands of women to fill positions of a basic operating nature. Business machine operators, secretaries, tellers, clerks—the overwhelming majority of such jobs nowadays are held by women.

But these by no means represent the only types of jobs available. Banks today have become much more conscious of their duties to the communities in which they operate and to their customers—duties of not only providing a safe place for savings and a source for loans, but of helping communities, businesses, and individuals make the most economical and wisest use of their assets. Women have shown themselves to be particularly gifted in meeting the public and in helping people with their financial planning and budgeting. Bankers have been giving more and more women an opportunity to utilize these talents.

At Bank of America women undertake important tasks in business development, loans, trust administration, public relations, advertising, training, and personnel. Many of these women, along with those who concentrate in the more traditional bank activities, are officers and executives. We currently have more than 3,582 women filling positions at official or semi-official levels such as assistant cashier in lending or operations, trust officer, business development officer and many others.

A Long Way To Go

Despite the immense strides women have taken into the business community in recent years, there is still a long and difficult road ahead.

Women's exposure to business has been very brief compared to the centuries men have been the merchants of the world. And learning the "tricks of the trade" takes a long time. Educational preparation is required. And you must also gain day-to-day experience on the job.

Moreover, there are a good many conflicting opinions—some objective and some clouded by emotion—that hinder a woman's progress in professional and business activities.

Some simply believe a woman's place is in the home and that's that. They say that in the fight to attain a professional position, a woman loses her femininity—that she is transformed into a harsh, ruthless, repellent person. Others argue that women have no patience; that they use their feminine wiles and tears and feign sickness to cover up their mistakes; that they don't understand company problems; that they take too much time off; and that they change jobs too frequently.

Yet there are certainly some ruthless businessmen; some who trade on their personality and charm to cover up lack of business ability. There are more than enough men who lose their patience or take time off due to illness. And there are many men who, once trained by a company, immediately leave for a better paying job.

In short, it is misleading to generalize about a person's fitness for employment strictly on the basis of gender. There are capable women as well as capable men and each individual must be judged on his or her demonstrated merits.

There is no question, however, that many segments of business are still reluctant to place women in executive trainee positions directly from college or in the early years of their life. Marriage, children, moving to follow her husband—these factors in particular have acted against a woman's chance for greater advancement.

Despite these drawbacks, there are more women than ever who are striving to make a success in business and who are patient with their progress. Many are seeking additional education in the evening at local schools, colleges, or through the American Institute of Banking. Attitudes have improved and women are encouraging younger women to set better examples of attendance, punctuality, appearance, and interest in the job.

Women are reading the same periodicals that men have found helpful in their advancement, and they are putting this knowledge to use. They realize that the problems of their home must be left there and that their jobs must be uppermost in their mind when they are at work.

Reaching The Top

Back in the twenties, a large New York bank decided to make a personnel change in its famous "Ladies Drawing Room." The room had been set up to serve the banking needs of wealthy women and had been completely staffed by men. Women customers did not seem to be seeking financial counsel as they should be, or making sufficient use of the bank's services. So, bank executives chose a young alert girl who had been a clerk to sit at a desk in the room and offer advice and guidance to women customers.

Her name was Dorothy M. Armbruster, and she was so successful that she eventually rose to vice president in the bank.

At Bank of America, there is another person who has become the symbol of women's ability to master big business. She is Mrs. Claire Giannini Hoffman, daughter of our founder, A. P. Giannini; and she is a member of our Board of Directors. She is also the first woman elected to the Board of Directors of Sears Roebuck and Company. The friends Mrs. Hoffman has won for Bank of America number in the thousands, and she has taken a great interest in assisting women to find a career in banking.

There are numerous other examples that prove women can go far and high in the business world. Mrs. Charles Ulrich Bay, who was president and chairman of the board of A. M.

Kidder and Company on Wall Street, said, "We lack sufficient women in top executive positions. The women of today have greater responsibility than ever before to contribute to leadership."

There can be no doubt that there is a place for the professional woman in today's labor market. Her brains and capabilities are too valuable to be wasted. Given the opportunity to develop her mind and ability, the modern woman can become a highly valued executive.

CHAPTER VI

Banking's Foreign Affair

The reign of Mutsuhito, one-time Emperor of Japan, began in 1867. At that point Japan was essentially a feudal country. In 1868, the Emperor committed the government to seek knowledge and wisdom throughout the world in order to enable his country to compete effectively with Western powers. A number of trade missions were organized to travel abroad and find knowledge which could be adapted to Japanese life.

For their constitution the Japanese found the German model suited them best. They framed a new judicial code based on the French Code Napoleon. The two major industrial innovations of that age were the advent of the railroad and the invention of the spinning machine. The Japanese relied on the English for these, and established commercial contacts with Great Britain in many other business fields as well. After the French defeat in the Franco-German war of 1870–71, the Japanese Navy tended to look upon Britain as a model, and in later years, to watch closely naval developments in the United States.

The results of this conscious search for know-how were startling. In less than 50 years, Japan emerged from a state of isolated feudalism to a major world power.

Today, the situation is no different. Skill, knowledge, and technique are prerequisites for development. A recent international conference, including leading citizens from many countries in the world, agreed that the most pressing need of underdeveloped nations is for managerial and technological know-how. Their second priority is for greater infusions of private capital. On another occasion, quite recently, an industrialist from an underdeveloped country told me with great fervor and sincerity of his people's gratitude for technological assistance. He said: "You could have just given us money, but you didn't. You invested in our country. You showed our people how to do things they did not know how to do, and in this way you preserved their pride and dignity. You made it possible for them to be self-supporting, and now they truly feel like partners in a great enterprise."

This emphasis on the need for managerial and technological skills should not be surprising. We know that a number of substantial long-term low-cost loans to developing countries have remained totally unused for the lack of technical knowledge. Large-scale financing and government grants will be of no avail to a people with little or no experience in an industrial economy. Lacking industrialization, they have neither the knowledge nor means to produce, nor the income to purchase. Hence, the overriding need to export from the United States what we popularly call "know-how."

American businesses, individually and collectively, are rising to this challenge.

Exports of Knowledge

Some time ago, International Business Machines Corporation opened a modern building on the campus of the University of Ibadan in Nigeria. Here IBM financed a two-year course for fifty students in such subjects as accounting, business law, economics, mathematics, and data-processing. The goal was to prepare the students for jobs in local industry and government and thus narrow the gap in business and technical training in Africa.

The program described in Nigeria is only one example of IBM's past or present efforts to export knowledge and skills. The management of this multinational corporation is well aware that the success of their overseas operations, which account for nearly half of total sales, is dependent on upgrading the skills of their 131,000 employees in foreign countries while at the same time training in the use and operation of their products the employees of business, industry and government who purchase them. Thus IBM is a major exporter of education as a support to manufacture and marketing. The means to accomplish this objective may be as simple as sponsoring a special educational unit in an established university or as sophisticated as The IBM European International Education Center of La Hulpe, Belgium.

In Africa and South America, United Brands Company and Castle and Cook, Inc., the great banana growers, have provided large scale aid to local private farmers. The companies have helped these farmers clear land; have assisted in the installation of irrigation and pesticide spray equipment; and have provided seed, stock, and fertilizers. This system is gradually supplanting the company-owned plantation as a source of supply. But it is doing something else vastly more important—it is creating agricultural competence, and of all the technology we can export, agricultural know-how is the most important. The underdeveloped country's greatest challenge is to create an agricultural revolution which will transform the peasantry from subsistence farmers to surplus farmers.

Sears Roebuck provides another example of enlightened American business overseas. Sears' policy has been to employ local people and create local suppliers. There are 51 retail stores and 23 retail sales offices operated by Sears' subsidiaries in Latin America with sales of nearly $338 million in 1974. Sears long standing policy has been that merchandise sold in Latin America should be produced there and that their employees should be almost exclusively natives of the countries in which they are doing business. In order to accomplish these objectives, Sears has helped local suppliers to manufacture products which meet their standards and conducts both extensive and intensive training and development programs for Sears stores and offices.

I could go on for some time citing examples of the way American business is responding to the technological problems of underdeveloped countries. It is an impressive story; a story that has not been told in the mass media; a story of which we can all be proud. And yet, the game is not without its risks. Doing business abroad is not for the timid or fainthearted. Once overseas, American businessmen will be faced with the myriad problems of operating in a foreign environment. The problems are not simply those implied by foreign trade regulations and markets—although these certainly must be understood to operate effectively. But the more difficult obstacles often have social or cultural implications—how to negotiate meaningfully with individuals whose entire heritage and traditions are totally different from, and in some cases totally contrary to, our own.

The Risks

Some of the pitfalls of operating overseas are tragic, but some, if we retain our sense of humor, are comic even when the joke is on ourselves. Take the case of Bank of America's branch in Paris. When we first bought our building there we decided, as a friendly gesture to the beautiful city of Paris, that we would clean up the exterior. Just about the time the job was finished, we were informed that we had "done wrong" since our building was a national monument and it now differed from the surrounding national monuments. Anxious to get off on the right foot with Parisians, we then re-dirtied our building in the most artistic manner possible. It was not long after that the city of Paris decided to *clean up* all its national monuments so—you guessed it—we set to work recleaning our building again.

This example, of course, reflects whimsically the nature of cultural and traditional clashes, but in our explosive world, the businessman overseas must face the harder problems of riot, bloodshed, and revolution. Let me cite another case from our files—the Cuban revolution.

When Fidel Castro assumed power, the flight of capital from Cuba tripled sales of Bank of America travelers cheques. This fact, plus the growing political instability, led us to the decision to close our Havana office in 1960. On August 7th of that year, Castro ordered the expropriation of all American investments in Cuba. At the time, we had two million dollars in blank travelers cheques on supply to Cuban banks that were literally as good as cash. As every ambassador knows, both in politics and in business, contacts are vitally important. Fortunately, the assistant representative in Bank of America's Mexico City office had such contacts in the Castro government.

He was quickly dispatched to Cuba, where his friend in the government gave local banks an "OK" to return the blank cheques to Bank of America. Our representative then had the unique job of burning $2 million worth of travelers cheques —in small batches so the secret police would not notice. The whole operation took ten days. A few weeks later, Castro nationalized all banks in Cuba.

On other occasions we have not been so fortunate. In 1947, Bank of America opened a Manila branch and helped the sugar industry stage a comeback. In April 1975, we closed the Saigon Branch in South Vietnam, a few days before the surrender of the city to the Communists. All personnel, including South Vietnamese, were evacuated by air to safety as the Viet Cong and the North Vietnamese took over.

Despite the problems posed by operating in a foreign climate and despite the risks of revolution and expropriation, American business overseas continues to rise, and the number of American businessmen and bankers traveling abroad increases with each passing year. Obviously, most of them have found it profitable.

The Rewards

In a recent calendar year, more than 155,000 passports were issued to United States citizens who were traveling abroad solely for business purposes. On an annual basis, one major international airline estimates that 30 percent of its passengers traveling abroad are American businessmen. Just how important are these men and the corporations they represent—just how important are their overseas missions to the growth of the total American economy?

Consider for a moment the American automobile business. It generates more than $77 billion a year. I'm sure you'll agree, this is big business.

United States exports amount to more than $91 billion per year; United States imports more than $90 billion. In total we are talking about a $181 billion import-export business—a business more than twice as large as the automobile industry.

The expansion of U.S. firms overseas since the close of World War II has been amazing. During one brief period, several years ago, more than 2,000 American companies ventured to establish new foreign operations. Most of the largest U.S. corporations now have operating facilities abroad. It has become customary to describe American corporations as either multinational or domestic in order to identify the extent of their operations. Obviously, international business must be good business and certainly the profit picture bears this out. Many major American companies now derive a substantial portion of their earnings from overseas operations. It is not unusual for 25 to 50 percent of net profits to arise from international activities. An example of the success of foreign operations is American Standard. This firm had total sales of more than $1,677 million in 1974. Of this figure 53 percent were domestic sales and 47 percent foreign. Product income was 64 percent U.S. and 36 percent from overseas. Colgate Palmolive Company, a name familiar to the American market-place, enjoys similar success from foreign operations.

Where Do Banks Come In?

It may seem we have strayed rather far afield from the basic topic of this book. But, indeed, we have not. Anyone's understanding of careers available in the modern banking industry would be woefully incomplete if he failed to examine closely current developments in the international field. Tomorrow's banking role in this field is related to the actions of today's businessmen. And their actions are related to overseas conditions. We have reviewed those conditions—foreign investment means high risks but even higher rewards. We have reviewed the American businessmen's reaction to those conditions—he is becoming more active internationally with each passing day. Now let's see how banks fit into the picture.

Suppose you are a manufacturer of cleaning goods and related products. You have watched your competitors, one by one, hop on the international bank wagon, and you have seen their total sales and income rise steadily as a result. You would like to get in on this new source of profits but hesitate for several reasons. The export market seems strange and complicated. You are not anxious to get involved in details, paper work, costly market studies, and so on. You wonder how to make proper contacts overseas—who will buy your product and resell it on the foreign market. How will you be assured of payment once you have shipped your goods? Will it be necessary to establish production facilities overseas and if so, how will you finance the expansion? These and a hundred other questions may plague the domestic manufacturer contemplating a venture into the international market.

The bank whose operation is already international in scope is in a unique position to assist such a manufacturer. It can familiarize him with documentary procedures and other technical aspects of the field; establish relationships with agents, distributors, or purchasers abroad; and work out investments or licensing arrangements overseas. It can provide current information about the business climate, trade regulations, and market conditions affecting various products in various areas abroad. If a manufacturer is considering establishing a foreign plant, the bank can provide guidance in obtaining authoritative data on labor conditions, wage levels, pertinent laws, taxes, and other related information. It can help the manufacturer to find reliable new sales outlets and sources of raw materials or finished products and can also help to evaluate markets for foreign expansion. To provide prompt reliable credit information in connection with foreign transactions, banks have access to valuable stores of data both in their domestic and overseas offices. In addition, they can call upon the credit information facilities of commercial houses and correspondent banks around the world.

Besides these *informational* services, the bank can also provide a manufacturer or other business representative *introductory* services. It can provide person-to-person contact with prominent businessmen, bankers, and government officials—people who will be important to success overseas, but people with whom it is extremely difficult to make contact because of complicated local protocol.

Finally, the bank can provide actual *credit* services. The wide range of international financing and refinancing methods includes letters of credit, trust receipts, warehouse receipts, and other instruments. Financing may also be arranged through advance accounts, trade acceptances, banker's acceptances, and the discounting of time drafts, providing buyers with extra time to arrange for payments and making funds immediately available to sellers when necessary. The forms required, many of the rules and regulations that apply, and even the terminology used in connection with these transactions are peculiar to the international field. Many of the procedures involved are not yet standardized to the point that electronic accounting can be used—so that much of the bookkeeping must be done manually. As a further complexity, almost all types of transactions handled in a bank's international department may involve any of the currencies used throughout the free world—from Argentine pesos or Guatemalan quetzals to Indian rupees or Danish kroner. Staff members must keep in mind the current exchange restrictions for each currency, as well as collection charges and any other charges that may be involved. Moreover, since incoming cables, letters, and documents are frequently written in the language of the originating country, no international department is complete without a full staff of translators.

The major career area in international banking involves performing the prime lending functions, developing new business, and maintaining contact and good relations with existing customers. You may work in the United States, providing expert financial assistance to firms either planning a foreign venture or already involved in one. Naturally, you will need the same broad credit experience that any bank lending officer must possess. But in addition, you will need a specialized knowledge of your customer's business—product—and requirements. More importantly, you will be required to have a thorough knowledge of the language, culture, customs, traditions, political philosophy and economic conditions in at least one foreign country You may actually be assigned to that country as a bank representative. It will then be your job to develop and maintain friendly relationships with local dignitaries, businessmen, officials, and other bankers. You will be expected to report regularly to your bank's domestic office any developments or changes that might affect the interests of the bank or its customers. You may also be asked to help prepare special reports on market potential, general economic conditions, or particular foreign industries for customers who are planning new overseas expansions. Finally, you may be assigned to a foreign branch to provide local customers with on the spot service . . . not only financial service but also informational service. For example, Bank of America's Paris branch might convey information relating to the common market to an exporter in China through one of our Hong Kong branches. Then when the exporter is ready to ship his goods, the two branches can handle the financial details of the transaction.

What's in Store?

The gains United States banks have made by getting into the international field in the past two decades are already on the books. Deposits in foreign branches have increased to around $100 billion of which approximately $8 billion is in demand and $93 billion in time accounts. Bankers acceptances drawn on and accepted by domestic banks primarily to finance imports, exports or the transfer or storage of goods in March of 1975 totaled $18,730 million. The number of overseas branches of United States banks increased from 95 in 1950 to 160 in 1965 and 700 in 1975. Bank-owned Edge Act and agreement corporations (corporations set up by banks for the purpose of investing in foreign industries) have increased from 6 in 1955 to 37 in 1965 and 116 in 1975 with total assets of more than $7 billion.

For some domestic banks, this rapid foreign expansion has

a familiar ring to it. Before 1913 they were prevented, for the most part, from setting up shop overseas. But once the law was changed, a number of United States banks rushed into the field. The 1920's, when trade and private investment were flourishing, saw a rash of American banks, dotted throughout the world, but a decade later they were forced by declining trade to retreat.

Now we are witnessing a new growth trend. It is one that bankers *can* and *must* help to preserve.

Can because bankers stand at the crossroads of this nation's commercial life. Their work brings them into daily contact with business leaders. Their advice is sought by the industrialist, the retailer, the contractor, and the investor. Bankers are thus in a unique position to encourage and assist American businessmen in responding to the great challenge posed by the underdeveloped nations.

Must for two reasons. First, the goal of increasing American business participation in the development of nations overseas is a practical one. These nations represent an enormously rich potential market for our goods and services. But the goal also has its ideological overtones in the world-wide conflict between capitalism and communism—in this battle for the sympathy and loyalty of uncommitted nations. At a conference Japan's former Prime Minister Hayato Ikeda made this observation: "Where there is no economic development, there is no abundant life. Where poverty exists, there is no general well-being. And today, when rapid expansion is taking place in economic and cultural relations between nations, no one nation can prosper unless others also prosper. Prosperity is indivisible. It is incumbent upon all of us, therefore, to go beyond our own national borders to contribute to the growth of the world's economy and to the enhancement of the welfare of mankind."

Here, then, is the principal reason bankers must encourage expanded foreign investment. In our explosive and restless world 70 percent of the people are nonwhite, two-thirds are non-Christian, and 95 percent are non-American. If we are to keep the peace and to help others and ourselves grow, we must break these barriers. To do less is to fail. Here, too, is why the field of international banking offers bright and growing prospects to today's young career-seeker. All in all, this is the area of banking that will undergo the largest, the most dramatic, and possibly the most challenging growth in the years ahead.

CHAPTER VII

Chart Your Course and Stick to It

Some years ago a friend of mine, now treasurer of a large San Francisco corporation, told me about a theme his nine-year-old son had written for a fifth-grade assignment. The topic was "What I Want To Be When I Grow Up," and the boy had indicated, somewhat to his father's dismay, that his life's ambition was to be a garbage man.

I asked what reasons the boy had given, whereupon the father produced his son's masterpiece and quoted directly from it: "When I grow up, I want to be a garbage man because I would get to ride on the back of a big truck. I would only work in the morning and I would only work three days a week. The rest of the time I could go swimming or play baseball or do anything I wanted to."

I told the father I thought the boy's remarks, in view of his present interests and his conception of what garbage men did, made a good deal of sense. Despite the lad's youth, he had been absolutely correct in his first step toward a career. He had taken stock of his own interests and desires, and compared them with what he felt to be the requirements of a certain field of work.

As the boy grew older, the wish to become a garbage man

faded, but oddly enough, no other particular career goal replaced it. He went through high school, then college, never knowing what he wanted to do. When it came time for him to embark upon a career, he took the first job offered, not bothering to examine it carefully. Six months later, he quit and took another job. This, too, proved unsatisfactory, and in less than year, he moved on to what he thought was a better position. From the time this young man graduated from college until the time he was thirty, he ran through seven jobs. Then he did what he had not done since the fifth grade. After assessing his abilities carefully and exploring possibilities open to him (much slimmer pickings than in the beginning because he was older now and had not established a stable record), he went to work as a floor salesman in a department store chain. Two years later, he was made buyer in his department and today, at thirty-five, he is manager of the store's entire sporting goods section.

This fellow was lucky; but hundreds of others who make the same mistakes he did never quite recover. Too many young people, about to enter the job market as self-supporting adults, expect some mystic power will suddenly reveal to them the ideal career. Or they think they will try a little of everything until they find the career that is just right. I do not recommend either method. Mystic powers are not much in vogue these days. And trying a little of everything is like eating all the relishes, appetizers, and rolls and then being too full to even taste the main course. While it is difficult to make a precise and definite career decision at an early age, you should not feel it is impossible to at least narrow down the field of alternatives.

This is not to say that you must make an irrevocable decision when very young. As you mature, your values and standards may change and the career that seemed perfect early in life may seem less so later on. But you can establish a firm and definite *direction*—by doing the same things our fifth grader did—examining your own interests and abilities and measuring them against several different fields of endeavor.

Balance Sheet for a Banker

The balance sheet, a document with which all bankers are familiar, is used to list and compare a company's assets and liabilities, thus showing its net worth. You can use the same principle to determine how much value your interests and natural aptitudes would be to you in a banking career. Each of the questions posed below should receive a yes or no answer. Consider "yes" an asset and "no" a liability. The difference between total yes answers and no answers is your "net worth" in terms of a banking career. The larger the number of yes answers, the better you will do in banking.

1. Do you get along well with people—can you be persuasive without being insulting, can you be polite to someone who is rude, are you poised and friendly in unfamiliar situations, can you be honest but diplomatic?
2. Do you like people and enjoy serving them regardless of their social status or background?
3. Are you a good judge of character—do you withhold your opinion until all the facts are available, do you avoid making snap judgments based on first impressions?

4. Do you have a general interest in business, finance, investment, and accounting?
5. Are you thorough and painstaking in your work—do you pay close attention to small details?
6. Are you willing to work long, hard hours and devote much of your "own" time to your job?
7. Are you willing to continue your education throughout your career—to participate in special training programs, to read regularly, perhaps even to attend night school or summer school?
8. Can you communicate with others—is your speaking and writing clear and comprehensible—can you make complex concepts understandable to the layman?
9. Are you willing to go through a period of internship, learning the more dull and routine aspects of the business and knowing that responsibility and more exciting assignments will come later?
10. Do you want to enter an industry that is growing and changing rapidly—one that requires you to grow and change with it?
11. Is discretion one of your strong points—can you keep confidential information confidential?
12. Do you possess a strong sense of civic pride and responsibility—do you wish to be an active and useful participant in the affairs of your community?
13. Do you wish to enter a field that will give you a bird's-eye view of many diverse types of enterprise and an opportunity to learn how each operates?

A yes answer to all or most of these questions makes banking a definite possibility on your career horizon. The next step is to review your *acquired* abilities and to determine how well they fit in with the needs of the banking industry.

Invest in Yourself

The story of the young person who graduates from high school; joins the local bank as a messenger; does a good job and is promoted to teller; then to head teller; then becomes assistant to the operations officer and takes over full operations responsibilities a few years later; is next offered an opportunity to train in the lending field; and ultimately winds up manager or president of the bank is not a myth. It can and does happen. But it is becoming a rarer and rarer story with each passing day. There is nothing so essential to today's potential banker as a broad college education in the social sciences and humanities. On the technical side, you should develop a firm grasp of economics, accounting principles, and statistics. If you want to move into the field of bank automation, a knowledge of mathematics will be mandatory. Moreover, your study of technical disciplines should be interspersed with large doses of the liberal arts: history, literature, and philosophy. Undergraduate schools and junior colleges which offer general business courses will usually include sufficient exposure to each of these fields. You should also seriously consider continuing your education beyond the undergraduate level. Though at the moment there is still an ample demand in the banking industry for those holding bachelor's degrees, it is likely that in the distant future, emphasis will be placed increasingly on advanced degrees in business and economics.

Do not assume, however, that a college diploma is a one-way ticket to success. There are diplomas and diplomas.

Those that are backed up by four years of mediocre scholastic performance, a lack of participation in school activities, and a record of misdemeanors and trips to the dean's office will do you about as much good as a subway token on an airplane.

Statistics show that the "greasy grind"—the person who is more interested in study and learning than in play, will end up going the farthest and earning the most in the business world. Next most successful is the campus leader—the person who was not the most brilliant student in the world but who played an active leadership role in campus affairs. Both types will do better in terms of salary and position than the campus nonentity—the person with no outstanding accomplishments.

Formal education, then, is the first and most important step in preparing for a banking career. But it is by no means the only step. There is also a great deal to be learned through independent research and reading. You will want to gain both a historical and a current, day-to-day perspective about banking. This is not really a difficult task. Public libraries have numerous books which describe the development of our banking system and define the functions banks perform in modern society. By subscribing to one of the many banking periodicals (See Appendix II) you can gain a good idea of what makes day-to-day news in the banking industry.

Finally, you can supplement your reading and study with actual work experience. A number of banks offer part-time summer jobs to young people of college age. A few have actual internship programs where you work successive summers, learning a different job each year. Naturally, this brief encounter with the business will not turn you into a full-fledged banker, but it will give you a much better idea of the manner in which a normal day's banking business is transacted. And it will give you a head start when you begin working full time.

The Recruiter's "Golden Rule"

What do bankers look for when they are hiring new employees? One of our recruiters at Bank of America summed it up in one sentence: *"We look to see how much a man has done with the opportunities presented."*

If you come from a wealthy family and have received an education without having to pay your own way, it will be expected that you have excelled academically or in terms of activities, or both. If you had to work your way through school, your academic accomplishments carry all the more weight. What have you done with your leisure time—your summers—your after-school hours? If you have been out of school for some time, what have you accomplished? What kind of leadership potential have you displayed? Have you willingly accepted responsibility when thrust upon you—have you eagerly sought responsibility in the areas where you have talent and skill? Are you aware of your weaknesses and how have you attempted to correct them? These will be the basic questions a recruiter will try to find answers to when interviewing you. And it is from these answers that the recruiter will be able to estimate how well you will do in a banking career.

There is a second set of questions almost as important. The recruiter will want to determine the strength of your motivation toward banking. Have you, on your own initiative, taken some steps to prepare yourself for a banking career? Do you know something about the banking industry? Remember, *you* may know what a talented, valuable employee you would make, but your employer can only judge on the basis of tangible evidence. Blind faith seldom plays an important role in the hiring decisions of a businessman. The recruiter must deal in facts, and the burden of proof rests with you.

Finally, your poise, appearance, personality, and personal traits will be taken into consideration. This does not mean you must put on a show of being a hearty, back slapping extrovert. Nor does it mean you must look as though you just stepped off a Hollywood screen set. It does mean, however, that you should be neat, clean, and courteous.

Finding a Fit

When you buy a new suit or a dress, you don't simply walk into a store, point to a rack, and say, "I'll take that one." Obviously, not all suits or dresses are alike—there are many different sizes, weaves, colors, and cuts. Some would fit and look good on you—others would not. The same is true of banks. In selecting the ones you would like to work for, you should make up a check list including the following points:

1. Size: We have already discussed the relative merits of large and small banks. You should weigh carefully the merits of each before making a decision.
2. Location: Climate, cost of living, housing, and general living conditions vary from one area of the country to another. Working conditions may also vary. Banks are usually open during the middle of the day; 10:00–3:00, 9:00–2:30, etc. However, in many localities, banks stay open for business until 5:00 or 6:00 P.M. on Fridays. Until relatively few years ago, banks usually were open

on Saturday mornings but this practice is less likely now. The place you decide to locate is not of major importance but should be a consideration.

3. Salary and Promotion: Information about a bank's entry level pay scales and salary review policies is difficult but not impossible to come by. Most banks review new employees' salaries annually. As a rule of thumb, you can assume your beginning salary at a large bank will be competitive with what you would receive at any major corporation. Smaller banks will usually pay somewhat less.
4. Training Programs: Many banks sponsor a number of specialized training and management programs designed to supplement the banking knowledge you have gained in college. Literature about these programs is generally available upon request.
5. General Background: Nearly every bank has a somewhat different general character. One may be highly conservative while another is liberal and progressive. Some may specialize in a particular phase of the business, such as trust services, while another devotes most of its energy to international banking. By studying a bank's annual reports, its advertising brochures, and any other publications it produces, you can gain a broad perspective of its "institutional personality." Again, these materials are usually available upon request.
6. Bonuses and Benefits: Banks on the whole have very generous employee-benefit plans when compared to other segments of private enterprise. As with salaries, it is sometimes difficult to obtain precise information about benefit plans, but you can usually discover at least whether or not the bank you are approaching has

some kind of overall plan. In some cases you will be able to determine just what the plan includes—medical insurance, life insurance, stock purchase options, retirement annuities, and so on.

The Approach

There are three basic ways to approach a prospective employer: through a personal contact, through a letter or phone call, or through a placement service or employment agency. Several years ago a study by one of California's major business schools showed that 54 percent of a recent graduating class made initial job contact through the school placement service; 18 percent used a letter or call; and 28 percent used a personal or family friend to establish contact, or went back to a previous employer. Thus, you can see that any or all of those techniques can be successful—it is a matter of adapting the proper technique to your situation.

Perhaps the most difficult approach is the letter. As a rule, you will have had no prior contact with the institution. You have no "in," no person in the bank who knows you or knows what you can do. Nevertheless, it is extremely important to address the letter to a particular bank officer, not simply to the institution. If you are dealing with a small bank, get the name of the president or vice president and direct your letter to that person. In a larger bank you can write the head of college recruiting or the employment division, or a senior officer in the particular department that interests you most. But again, take the trouble to get the officer's name and direct your letter to that person.

Make the letter short, cordial, and typewritten. In a few sentences you should indicate why you are interested in banking. A few more sentences should describe why you have selected the particular bank. Finally, ask if the officer would have time to visit with you for a few minutes—at a mutually convenient time. Remember bankers are busy and usually have a full calendar of appointments.

With the letter, enclose your resume. It should be one, or at the most, two type-written pages in outline form. List your educational background, age, marital status, and any work experience you have had. Emphasize any aspects of your work, educational, or military experience that you feel may be of value in a banking career. But, a word of caution, the resume is not an advertisement—it is a concise, factual portrait of yourself. Most bankers will see through any artificial embroidery; those who do not will be disappointed when they meet you and discover you look better on paper than in person. Perhaps the most important part of the resume will be the statement of your objective. Make this short—a couple of sentences should do—but make it as precise as you possibly can. Bankers like to meet young people who know where they are going. Finally, do not enclose with your letter any special citations or letters of recommendation. These can be produced later on if requested.

Your letter will be quickly answered and your request for an interview either refused or granted. If refused, reasons will be given. If granted, follow up with a short letter confirming the time and date of the appointment and thanking the officer.

When you are relying on a personal friend or placement service to establish contact with a prospective employer, they will usually set up an interview for you. Be certain they are supplied with your resume and whatever references they may request. They should forward them to the employer before your interview.

The Interview

There is no formula for guaranteeing a successful interview. There are, however, a number of precautions, a number of preparatory measures you can take to give yourself a better than even chance of making a good impression. Be on time and be neatly dressed. If you have done your homework, you should know something about the bank your interviewer represents. This knowledge should help you in two ways: you will be able to relate your own interests and talents to the needs of the bank; and you should have some questions about the bank that go beyond surface generalities. By asking those questions, you will help convince the interviewer that your interest in and knowledge of the bank is more than just casual.

In the strictest sense of the word, the initial interview with a prospective employer is not really a job interview. It is more an exploratory session. It is an opportunity for you to find out more about the bank and the bank to find out more about you. Topics such as salary, benefits and so on are out-of-bounds unless the interviewer introduces them. For the most part, the interviewer will try and draw you out. You may receive a general picture of starting salary ranges but it is not likely that a specific figure will be named. The conversation may move over a broad range of topics until one is found in which you are particularly interested. Then, it is likely that the interviewer will sit back and listen. The objective, especially in an initial interview, is to gain a general impression of your personality, motivation, and powers of communication. The interviewer will try to determine how well you put your education and knowledge to use in a spontaneous situation.

Do not expect the first interview to close with a job offer.

This happens rarely. If the interviewer has decided that you would be a good employee, there are steps to be accomplished in the employment process; references must be checked and decisions made as to salary and training appropriate to your background and experience. The result should be a carefully thought out offer that will be attractive to you.

Regardless of what you feel will be the outcome of your interview, follow-up with a note to your interviewer. If you were impressed with the interview, the opportunities described to you and would like very much to receive an offer of employment, don't hesitate to say so. One note of caution is appropriate however; don't overdo your appreciation for this often sounds insincere. If you were turned off during the interview and don't want to work for that bank or perhaps for any bank, write a thank you note anyway. It is just good business and common courtesy to express appreciation for the time and willingness to let you present your case for employment.

Plan of Action

It is most important that the young career-seeker form concrete objectives and goals before hunting a job in earnest. Failure to do so is like setting out on a long trip with no planned route or road map. Goals and objectives can change, of course, but at no time should you merely be drifting aimlessly. I am reminded of the young man who came to me several years ago seeking a position in our public relations department. He was a humanities major, fresh out of college, and had no particular knowledge of banking or public relations but thought he would "like to give it a try." His academic and activities records were fair and he seemed a nice enough person, but because he had no strong feeling about the contributions he could make to the bank and no specific future goals, I did not feel we should hire him.

A year later I had a letter from the same man. He had gone to work writing advertising for a newspaper. While the job paid well and offered him a chance to use his writing ability, he said his daily routine lacked variety. He had very little opportunity to deal with other people, almost no administrative responsibility, and no authority over others. Moreover, the chances of moving from his present position into these areas were slim indeed.

In looking for another job he had been struck by several features of the banking business. First, bankers come into daily contact with a wide variety of people. Second, he noted, a large proportion of banking jobs are supervisory or official in nature. Third, bankers must be articulate in expressing themselves—a skill he already possessed. He proposed that he come to Bank of America as a trainee in one of our branches—that he spend whatever time necessary learning the basic techniques of the banking business. Then later on he could be moved into the public relations department. His special talents could be put to use there; and because most people in that department have newspaper rather than banking backgrounds he would help to balance out the difference. Within a week he had been hired.

The Road to Excellence

Though most of our focus has been on *getting* a job, I cannot resist closing this chapter with a few words about *keeping* a job or, more important, making good on a job. I am not going to reveal any secret to success—I doubt that such a thing exists. But I would like to list six points I feel are vital to proper performance in your chosen career whether it be banking or anything else.

1. Always set the highest standard for yourself. Vow to do your job better than it has ever been done before. Promise yourself that you will better all your predecessors on your job and set a standard that your successor will have to really scramble to meet.
2. Work hard and efficiently. Remember that any task is 90 percent perspiration and 10 percent inspiration. But be sure that the perspiration is not wasted. Organize your work and your day for maximum efficiency. Remember that work can only be measured by results.
3. Dig deeper for facts. Look beyond what has been done before for the additional fact, the added statistic which can change the whole problem equation.
4. Think harder. Don't fall into the easy trap of accepting established patterns as the only way to do a job. Use your resourcefulness to find new approaches. Look for more efficient methods. Be on the lookout for new services to develop and new ways to serve. And then speak out for the better methods you see.
5. Remember the human equation. Make more friends among your associates and customers. Make people like to deal with you because you are more pleasant, helpful, and genuinely interested than anyone they know.
6. Be courageous and tough minded—call a spade a spade. In setting standards of performance, have the courage to point out a person's faults—fairly, honestly, but above all, unequivocally. Don't beat around the bush in your

counseling. Offer encouragement, but cite clearly—looking the person in the eye—what is wrong and what you expect. To do less is to fail as a manager of people and to fail the people you manage.

CHAPTER VIII

The Pot of Gold

Banking is a growth industry. It expands with the economy. In 1900, for example, there were about 10,000 banks in the United States. Their combined deposits totaled less than $9 billion. Today, we have some 14,500 banks with over 28,000 branch offices. Total deposits are over $400 billion. Because of these extensive facilities Americans can and do write more than twenty-six billion checks a year amounting to more than $13 trillion.

What does this growth mean to the young career seeker? First of all it means jobs. There are approximately 1.1 million people employed in banking. Approximately 1 out of 5 employees is an officer or about 220,000 total officers of which one-sixth are women. Each year thousands of employees move up to supervisory and official status. It has been estimated that one thousand new chief executive officers are needed each year. In almost no other industry is the route upward open to so many young people. According to the "Occupational Outlook Handbook, 1974–75 edition published by The U.S. Department of Labor, employment for bank personnel "is expected to increase rapidly through the 1980's."

An important corollary of this demand is salary. To get

their fair share of qualified young people, banks must be willing to pay—and pay they do.

Scratch One Myth

It has long been said, and believed, that banking is a low-paying industry. This may have been true once, but today it is pure myth. As more skills and specialities have been required to improve and modernize banking, salaries have increased accordingly. More than one study has uncovered this fact.

It is equally true that banking is not one of the highest paying industries. Banking salaries fit somewhere in the middle of the scale between the highest and the lowest paid employees in our country. However, when we are describing banking practices and policies in general terms, we are including the whole range of banks from smallest to largest. Many unit banks serving very small communities have as few as five or ten employees. The major banks in large cities either with or without satellite or statewide branches require hundreds or even thousands of employees to carry on their operations. Of course, salaries paid differ from the smallest to the largest banking firms, just as the responsibilities and complexities of the delivery of bank services varies from big to little banks.

A factor which should not be over-looked when comparing bank salaries with the salaries paid by others in the business community is that they are less likely to be affected by business trends. Although bankers' salaries usually do not move up rapidly when the economy is on the upswing, they customarily do not move down or move very slowly when the economy is in trouble. Layoffs or terminations due to recessions or depressions, contrary to the practice of most industrial firms, have been confined to a few banks. These few institutions have been poorly managed or located in severely depressed areas.

If you are concerned about salary, it is advisable to shop around. Interview firms in a variety of business activities. Next interview large banks and small ones, community institutions and big city operations and finally unit banks as well as major branch systems. If you keep good records of the information derived from your interviews, you should be able to make accurate comparisons between entry salaries paid by the banks and other business activities as well as those paid by the different types of banking institutions. Do not make your decision based solely on entry salaries. It is important to also look at long range salary prospects, general opportunities, working conditions and where you will have to live. Then make your decision.

Second Growth

We have seen in general that banks and bank salaries are growing. But there is a second kind of growth, equally important to your career: that is the growth of you as an individual. As a banker you will be exposed to a wide range of supervisory and advisory positions—most are complex in nature—and all carry with them a heavy burden of responsibility. As you progress in your career, your capacity to take on the next higher job will depend upon the extent of additional training and education with which you equip yourself. Most modern banks recognize this and have set up their own internal programs for training and development. In other words, they not only hire and pay you, they also enable you to move ahead in your career by training you.

Bank of America, for example, has offered special management training programs since 1947. Outstanding college and university graduates are selected for career development and trained in general banking as well as in the specialized functions typical of a large banking institution. The objective of these programs is to provide opportunities for early assignment to positions of responsibility. A typical program would consist of the following:

1. Work Assignments: Practical training is received through work assignments in branches and departments in administration. The work is both stimulating and challenging, and is carefully planned to provide excellent developmental experience.
2. Supervision: A bank officer calls on each trainee at regular intervals in the branch or administration department where he is receiving training. Together they review the trainee's progress and his future assignment. Time is provided for special coaching, counseling, and guidance.
3. Supplemental Study: Training received through working assignments is supplemented by study of related texts on banking and finance. The objective is to learn the language of banking and to provide a background of knowledge to support work performed. Examinations are given at regular intervals so that both the trainee and the supervisor may evaluate progress attained.
4. Seminars and Workshops: In addition to practical training, experience and supplemental study, special meetings and seminars are conducted for trainees at regular intervals. Subject matter which is presented is directly

> related to the objectives of training and development. Sessions are well balanced between lectures and discussions. Audio-visual aids are used to assist in presenting the material in a more interesting and informative manner.

Despending upon his background and skill, the participant in such a program can expect to become an officer of Bank of America within a relatively short time after joining the institution. Naturally, not all bank training programs follow the same pattern. An institution will try to adapt its training to its needs. Some offer accelerated electronic data processing courses to selected candidates with appropriate college majors and strong aptitude for this type of work. Some offer special instruction in bond and trust investment with assignment to one of the two areas upon completion of training. Men with Master's degrees in business administration may receive accelerated training in investments or corporate finance while those who have extensive business experience before entering banking will be given a telescoped program which focuses only on those areas with which they have not had prior contact.

To a limited extent, there are also training programs available for high school graduates who have had several years of business experience prior to entering the banking field. These people receive on-the-job training in junior supervisory positions. If they show a high degree of competence and perseverance, their opportunities to advance to positions of responsibility are excellent. But as they move up in the bank, they will be competing to an increasing extent with college graduates. They are therefore sometimes compelled to compensate for this educational difference by working a little harder and showing a little more initiative.

The American Institute of Banking offers the young banker still another opportunity to advance his career at an early age. A non-profit organization, AIB was established in 1900 as an educational arm of the American Bankers Association. Today it has 730 chapters or study groups, 961 correspondent students, nearly 200,000 members and approximately 100,000 enrollments scattered throughout the United States.

AIB's instructors are experienced professionals, especially recruited from among leading bankers, lawyers, and accountants and from among teachers in high schools, colleges, and universities. First level courses include Effective English, Principles of Bank Operations, Commercial Law, Negotiable Instruments, and Economics. Effective English is designed to help you speak and write correctly. Principles of Bank Operations is a study of the principles and function of commercial banking. It stresses the why of banking functions and explains the principles involved for both small banks and large. In other words, the student looks at banking from the viewpoint of the beginner: first, the banking functions; second, banking services; third, control of banks; and finally, banking's role in community life—both yesterday and today.

Commercial Law is offered to the student so he will have an idea of what is law and what is not. The especially prepared textbook—as are all AIB texts—cites ruling cases on various points of law applicable to banking. Negotiable Instruments deals with the provisions of the Uniform Negotiable Instruments Law and the newer Uniform Commercial Code. The law of negotiability, which for a long time was confined to checks and promissory notes, has been extended in accordance with business demands to bills of lading, stock certificates, bonds, certificates of deposit, trade acceptances, bank acceptances, and warehouse receipts. Knowledge of himself is vital to anyone who considers himself a banker.

The Economics course approaches the subject from the problem standpoint. Among the subjects discussed are the human and natural resources of the economy; the impact of science and technology; iron and steel, coal, and oil industries; farm problems; manufacturing industries; railroads; and public utilities. The more significant economic trends of recent years are also analyzed so that the student will have a foundation for understanding the present economic picture.

These then are some of the elementary courses available. As you advance to the graduate level of AIB, the areas of study become progressively more complex and specialized. Moreover, you will find that there are other specialized banking schools readily available to you. Technical banking courses are offered by the Stonier Graduate School of Banking, in cooperation with Rutgers University, the School of Banking at the University of Wisconsin, the School of Banking of the South at Louisiana State University and the Pacific Coast Banking School at the University of Washington. These courses are usually sponsored jointly by the educational institutions involved and various banking associations, and most of the students attending are sent by their banks as a part of career development. Quite frequently, AIB courses, which are far more accessible to the average young banker, will be paid for in part or in total by your employer.

On the Fringe

Fringe benefits, once regarded by some as a revolutionary and dangerous concept, have become as common today as apple pie. And nowhere have they gained a stronger foothold than in the banking business. Bankers enjoy excellent fringe benefits that provide them and their families with health care, both disability and life insurance, pensions and profit-sharing plans that are among the best and most comprehensive in business and industry. For example:

1. Life Insurance: After a certain period of time, usually six months to a year, the bank that employs you may purchase a life insurance policy for you. The amount is usually determined by your salary—as it increases so will the face value of your policy. Some banks also make it possible for you to buy a small policy on members of your family. In some instances you pay half the premium costs—in others, you may pay nothing.
2. Hospitalization, Surgical, and Major Medical Insurance: Many banks offer their employees and employees' families full medical coverage at greatly reduced insurance rates.
3. Profit-Sharing: A certain amount of a bank's yearly earnings may be invested in an employee's profit-sharing fund. The interest and dividends that accrue are then held in trust for employees until they reach retirement age. The extent to which you participate in such a plan usually depends upon your seniority, your salary, or both.
4. Retirement Plan: Beyond a certain age you will be eligible to participate in your bank's employee retirement plan, a fund from which you receive fixed monthly payments after retirement. You may make regular contributions to this fund over the years or the bank may make them for you.
5. Miscellaneous: You may receive other benefits including paid sick leave and paid vacations. Some banks will make their services available to you without charge,

including free checking accounts and free travelers cheques. In many cases you may borrow at preferred interest rates for the purchase of homes, furnishings, automobiles, etc.

The Long View

Banking promises a number of other less obvious rewards —rewards that will become increasingly important to you as you become more firmly established in your career. First, banking has an ancient and honorable heritage. Traditionally, it has been known as an honest, respectable profession, participated in by people of high integrity, sound principles, and common sense. Association with such a profession will gain you respect and prestige among your friends and other members of the business and professional community.

Because nearly every town in the United States has at least one bank—and because there is very little variation in procedures and regulations—banking offers you a high degree of mobility. Once you have mastered the basic principles, you can pursue your career in almost any state, any city you wish.

And do not overlook the consideration of stability and security. Banks have a better record in these areas than almost any other industry. For one thing, they deal in a commodity that is apt to be around for some time: money. Because, in most cases, it is other people's money, banks have over the years adopted steady and conservative policies. Moreover, they have come under the close observation and regulation of state and federal governmental agencies. This means that the industry as a whole will react more slowly and less violently to any drastic swings in the national economy.

Your job as a banker is less likely to be threatened by sharp downturns or recessions in economic activity.

There is still one more set of rewards to be considered. We live in an age when one hears much of the word "exchange." Cultural exchanges, educational exchanges, governmental exchanges—all are put forth as effective ways to promote better world understanding. I agree. And I would like to focus for a moment on the bank's role in modern society as an agent of exchange.

In the beginning it was probably the development of money, a medium of exchange, that led to the necessity for banks, the agents of exchange. When one person wished to sell and another to buy, it was a bank that facilitated the transaction. In essence, the bank was merely coordinating the needs of one person with those of another—at first on a limited geographical scope involving a limited number of people.

As banks began to extend their services to more types of people—to the poor as well as the wealthy, to the unfortunate as well as the privileged, to laborers as well as landowners—bankers began to see what an important role they could play in raising the general standard of living. Education, housing, household goods, and appliances were put within reach of many more people than ever before. Today, bankers continue to play such a role. And it is a source of much reward.

As banks began to spread geographically—bringing the wealth of urban centers into rural areas—bankers gained another new insight. They watched how the funds they brought with them from wealthy cities were used to improve small towns and rural areas. New schools sprang up; agriculture was modernized and made more productive; libraries, parks, better roads, and newer homes were built. Helping these small communities develop and improve has also been a source of reward to the modern banker.

Finally, as banks have crossed the oceans and entered foreign lands, they have shouldered still a greater and more awesome responsibility. Bankers are no longer involved only with the needs of domestic individuals and communities. They are now concerned also with the needs of entire nations, entire populations in other countries.

And decisions to exercise their option as exchange agents have become increasingly complex. Political, cultural, and social considerations as well as basic economic factors must play a role in the modern banker's decision-making process. Yet he must meet these challenges with all the skill he can command, because a transaction or exchange that begins as merely economic can quickly become a social benefit—the foundation for a more important exchange—the exchange of ideas.

In today's fast-moving and troubled world, the thought that bankers can play some small part in increasing understanding and prosperity among people of all nations, all classes, is perhaps the greatest reward of all.

APPENDIX I

Glossary of Bank Services

DEPOSIT SERVICES

Checking Accounts:

A checking account lets you pay bills the quick, convenient, economical way—by mail. Checkbook stubs provide a record of expenditures, help you plan and control a budget. Your cancelled checks, returned to you, are positive proof of payment. You can open an Individual Account or a Joint Account for use by two or more persons. Monthly service charges are based on your balance, and on the number of checks you write. This charge can be reduced or avoided altogether simply by increasing your balance.

Special Checking Accounts:

A special checking account is ideal if you write only a few checks each month. Simply open an account and deposit any amount you wish. No minimum balance is required, and charges are nominal.

Savings Accounts:

An Individual Savings Account is an all-purpose accumulation account. Use it for saving the down payment on a home, for college expenses, funds for future investment, to set up housekeeping, or pay for baby's arrival. Your account will earn regular bank interest. Many banks also offer special savings accounts and savings certificates at higher interest rates. Joint Savings Accounts are the same except that they are carried by two or more persons, and withdrawals may be made by any one of them—on one or more signatures, as arranged. In the event of death, title to the account passes automatically to the survivors upon proper release from tax authorities.

Christmas Club Savings Accounts:

To save the sum you'll need for Christmas shopping—or for such year-end expenses as taxes and insurance premiums—simply set your savings goal and make deposits regularly during the year. Then, before the holiday season begins, you'll receive a Christmas Club check for all you've saved plus interest.

Allotment Savings Accounts:

Members of our armed forces at home or abroad can arrange with finance or disbursing officers to put aside part of their monthly pay for deposit in a Savings Account.

School Savings Accounts:

Some banks offer young people an opportunity to develop the habit of thrift through the systematic saving of a few cents or more each week. Interest is paid on balances of any size.

Trustee Savings Accounts:

Trustee Savings Accounts may be established by parents or guardians as trustees for children. Provisions are the same as for other Savings Accounts, except that only the trustee may withdraw funds.

Public Funds—Demand and Time:

Most banks welcome Demand and Time Deposits from the state, counties, cities, irrigation districts, municipal water districts, and other governmental agencies. These banks furnish immediate collateralization of public funds and render assistance in investment programs for public entities.

GENERAL CUSTOMER SERVICES

Safe Deposit Boxes:

You can keep valuable possessions and important papers in a Safe Deposit Box. Bank Vault Space may be rented by the month to store furs, silverware, and other valuables. Many banks also provide Night Depository Service, enabling customers to make deposits after banking hours, on weekends and holidays.

Installment Collections:

The collection of rents and other regularly recurring obligations can be made efficiently and economically by a bank. The money received is either credited to your account or sent to you in accordance with your instructions.

Money Orders—Cashier's Checks—Bank Drafts:

Money Orders may be purchased at most banks in amounts up to $300. In many cases, attractive gift envelopes are furnished without charge for use on special occasions. Cashier's Checks are for larger amounts. Both are recommended for use only in your home state. Bank Drafts may be used to send payments outside the state.

Automatic Transfer of Funds:

You may authorize an Automatic Transfer of Funds—on regular dates—to any savings accounts or loan accounts you have at your bank. This service can carry out your intention to save money regularly, protect you against forgetfulness, and save you many trips to the bank.

Travelers Cheques:

Travelers cheques are honored everywhere—at banks, hotels, gas stations, resorts, department stores, both at home and abroad. These convenient self-identifying cheques protect your travel funds against loss or theft. Buy them at banks everywhere.

LOAN SERVICES

Automobile Financing:

Low-cost automobile financing can easily be arranged through leading dealers in your community or at your local bank. An installment loan may be used to buy a new or used car, to buy tires, a radio, or other accessories, to repaint, or pay for repairs. In addition, you may obtain a loan on your present car, whether paid for or not, through many banks. No co-signer or guarantor is required.

Household Appliance Financing:

Refrigerators, television sets, radios, hi-fis, pianos, ranges, washers, furniture—these are only a few of the household items that are easily financed through dealers in your community. Arrangements are made in the store, at the time you make your purchase, or at your bank.

Personal Loans:

Some expenses are unforeseen, like medical bills or auto repairs. Others, such as taxes, can be underestimated. Debts can accumulate. Personal Loans are available to meet such emergencies.

Doctor-Patient Loans:

Medical, dental, and hospital services can be paid for in convenient monthly installments through low-cost loans. In many cases, you can make arrangements right on the spot—in any hospital, medical, or dental office. It's an increasingly popular way to finance health care.

Professional Term Loans:

This special loan program is designed to help dentists and medical doctors meet the burdensome cost of starting or updating their professional practices. Rates are low and terms are convenient.

Educational Loans:

Banks offer these loans to finance all or any part of a college education, graduate studies, professional training, even preparatory schooling. In effect, educational loans put the cost of education—tuition, travel, living expenses and so forth—on a convenient month-to-month basis.

United Student Aid Fund Loans:

Some banks participate in this low-cost educational program that enables students to borrow funds for their college educations in cases where the terms of standard educational loans do not fit their needs. Students should check with their school Financial Aid Officer to determine if their college or university participates in the program.

Home Modernization and Improvement Loans:

These loans provide low-cost financing for alterations, repairs, and modernization—for almost any type of improvement to your home, inside or out, from roof to foundation, from redecorating to landscaping.

Mobile Home Loans:

These popular loans make modern, low-cost housing mobile homes and travel trailers available to an increasing number of families.

Marine Equipment Loans:

Boats, motors, boat trailers, and other marine equipment—for pleasure purposes—can be readily financed through a bank.

Savings and Loan Association Accounting Services:

Mortgage Loan Accounting Service handles all of the regular loan accounting functions required by Savings and Loan Associations: posting payments, calculating interest, and preparing regular certifications. In addition, the bank traces delinquent loans, performs insurance follow-up, provides accounting and statistical information for management and regulatory agencies. Special reports can be furnished for groups of loans serviced for, or owned jointly with, other lenders.

Share Savings Accounting handles all necessary records and notifications required to prepare and maintain accounts of this nature. An interesting by-product of the service is the entirely automatic preparation of government Form 1099, an information return.

Business Services Payroll can produce payroll checks, tax reports, and all necessary records from basic data supplied by the Savings and Loan Association. A number of special management control reports covering labor distribution are also made available.

Crop Production Loans:

Banks help thousands of farmers throughout the country meet the cash outlays required in the planting, growing, harvesting, and marketing of the nation's commercial crops.

Farm Equipment Loans:

Farmers can finance the purchase of tractors, implements, and other production and harvesting machinery through many banks. Payments are geared to farm income. Inventory financing is available to farm equipment dealers.

Livestock Loans:

People who make a business of dairying or raising beef cattle, sheep, and poultry find that banks can tailor a financing plan suited to their seasonal needs.

Intermediate Term Loans:

Crop and livestock producers occasionally need to make certain capital investments to further growth and development. While profits from one season's income may not be sufficient to handle the obligation, a realistic two- or three-year repayment plan may be negotiated at some banks.

Real Estate Loans:

Banks lend money to buy or build homes, apartment houses, stores, and other improved properties. Loans to buy or improve farm property are also available. Real property may also be used to secure long-term loans for other purposes.

Commercial Loans—Unsecured:

These loans are made to individuals, business firms, and other organizations on the basis of their financial responsibility. They are made for periods ranging from 30 days to a term of years for the purpose of assisting production, carrying inventory, meeting seasonal needs for working capital, and other requirements.

Commercial Loans—Secured:

The only difference between these loans and those mentioned in the above paragraph is that they are secured by listed stocks, bonds, warehouse receipts, or other acceptable collateral.

Term Loans to Small Business:

Some banks have a special loan plan for starting, buying, or expanding small businesses. These loans may be secured. Terms are geared to the firm's earnings.

Industrial Equipment Loans:

Equipment financing is available through many banks for the purchase of all types of income producing machinery, including shop equipment, and for construction equipment of all kinds. Customers can also obtain loans on their equipment to finance other projects beneficial to their business.

Truck Loans:

Loans for the purchase of new or used trucking equipment can be arranged through most banks. Loans can also be obtained by individual truckers or trucking companies on their equipment to finance consolidation, expansion, or for other worthwhile business purposes.

Aircraft Loans:

Aircraft of many types can be financed through many banks. These loans can be particularly useful to businesses which require considerable travel to supervise and service large territories.

Accounts Receivable Financing—Factoring:

Accounts Receivable Financing provides flexible working capital for manufacturers, wholesalers, and jobbers by making available to them, without interruption of regular routine, cash invested in receivables. This service is also available to large retail department stores to finance their revolving and open accounts. *Factoring* is essentially the same service except that accounts receivable are purchased outright. It relieves the seller of all credit risk, collection and bookkeeping expense. In addition, it provides a self-liquidating source of working capital.

Commercial Property Improvement Loans:

These loans are particularly important to apartment house and commercial property owners as well as to owners of all types of income producing property. They provide owners with funds to modernize, repair, alter, and enlarge their holdings—and at the same time, keep their properties at peak earning potential. In this way owners can avoid tying up capital or increasing mortgages.

Indirect Collections:

Through this service banks lend to stores and business organizations a portion of the money owed them on retail sales contracts. This streamlined service provides a steady flow of working capital at nominal cost. At the same time, since customers make their payments at the store, continuous contact between the dealer and his customers is maintained.

Inventory Distribution Financing Plan:

I.D.F. Plans make it possible for a manufacturer to distribute inventories to his customers at the times, and in the quantities, most favorable to his production capacity. It also enables his customers to stock larger inventories than they might normally obtain on an open account basis. The manufacturer simply agrees to repurchase the inventory if necessary, and credit is extended to the customer secured by the inventory. Manufacturer and customer alike enjoy improved cash position and sales potential.

Commodity Loans:

These loans are made to producers, processors, manufacturers, distributors, and dealers, and are secured by all types of readily marketable commodities, raw materials, and in some instances, finished goods.

Leasing:

Some banks now offer full services in the field of equipment lease financing. Any type of capital equipment—computers, construction equipment, electronic equipment, machine tools—can be acquired by the bank for leasing to customers over fixed terms at negotiated money costs. Requirements as to specifications, price, and delivery are handled between vendor and user exactly as if purchase were contemplated. The equipment is delivered to the customer and carries the same guarantees, warranties, and services as a regular purchase. The bank owns the equipment and the customer enjoys its use.

BUSINESS SERVICES

Time Deposits—Open Account and Certificates:

Interest-bearing accounts are provided by banks for corporations, partnerships and other organizations excluded by law from holding regular savings accounts. *Time Deposits: Open Account* have many features similar to savings accounts, including a passbook record and provision for additional deposits under the same contract. *Time Certificates of Deposit* are instruments covering deposits of stated amounts. Deposits in each type of accounts are made for specific periods of time, with the interest rate determined by the time interval. Banks offer a wide range of terms and renewal options which can be tailored to suit business and individual cash-flow requirements.

Business Services Payroll:

From basic data supplied by the employer, banks produce payroll checks, tax reports, and all necessary records. A variety of special management control reports are also available covering labor distribution.

Collections:

Obligations supported by documents, which are due business concerns and individuals, are collected and deposited to the customer's account by many banks.

Domestic Credit Information:

Some banks can provide accurate and unbiased credit data from any community in the state or across the nation.

Regional Collection Plan:

For firms of all types, this service—by rapidly converting regional receivables into working dollars—can reduce exposure to potential credit losses, allow closer control of bank balances, and cut down clerical office work.

Bank Wire Service:

For customers of the more than 253 bank-wire member banks, located in the principal financial centers of the nation, this service is of great value in effecting telegraphic payments, handling urgent credit inquiries, bond transactions and other priority matters.

Community Development:

Banks sometimes provide information for the local community that wants to make itself more attractive as a place to live, visit, or invest in. This includes assistance on analysis of the economic advantages, business climate, housing and recreational facilities of the area. Material is available on industrial development, economic base studies, land for industry, and a variety of other subjects.

Plant Location Service:

Some banks provide authoritative and objective aid in locating plant sites, distribution centers, warehouses, and research facilities, and other types of industrial real estate throughout the local area.

Industrial Investment Services:

Information gathered from close contacts with key executives in finance and industry enables some banks to offer a unique advisory service to U.S. industries and individuals interested in acquisitions, mergers, or investments in local companies.

Account Reconciliation Service:

This service is particularly valuable to business firms using a thousand or more checks per month. MICR imprinted paper checks are processed on modern computer equipment to provide a daily register of checks paid and a monthly certification register of all checks issued, checks outstanding, stop payments, and cancellations with all related totals. A number of options are available with this service to provide flexibility in meeting individual requirements.

Business Services—Freight Payment:

For shippers and receivers of goods shipped by common carrier, this service reduces the cost of handling accounts payable and provides automatic compliance with the regulatory time limits for freight bill payment. For carriers, the service reduces the costs of handling receivables and assures faster collections. Freight bills deposited by carriers are credited immediately to their accounts and debited to the accounts of shipper members. This cuts check-writing costs for shippers and provides more time for their audits. Shippers retain full control, because any disputed charge is promptly reversed.

Billing Service:

All phases of receivables are processed for utility-type industries. Included are billing, cashiering, individual customer accounting, and management control reporting. Virtually any industry having repetitive type accounts receivable billings can save money and improve management control by using the service.

Employee Loan and Deposit Service:

If you have a plant, regional office or other facility, this plan enables you to provide a sound and convenient method of banking for your employees—at no loss of working time or pay. Employees can arrange loans and deposits without leaving the plant or office.

TRUST SERVICES

Executor or Co-Executor of Wills:

As Executor of your will, a bank insures that your wishes are carried out without interruption—for a bank has a continuing existence and, unlike an individual, is never sick or away from business. Money is collected, debts and taxes are paid, and your estate is managed efficiently, with the least possible cost and expense. This experienced, professional service costs no more than an individual executor is entitled to receive under the law. Banks will also act as Co-Executor with a person of your choice who is intimately acquainted with your affairs. In addition, if a person should die without leaving a will or without naming an executor—or if the executor named fails to act—a bank may be appointed Administrator of the estate if nominated by the heirs.

Probate Agency:

A Probate Agency provides complete estate management. Practically all of the services performed when a bank acts as Executor of an estate, including all detail and accounting, are available to individual executors and administrators.

Trustee or Co-Trustee Under Wills:

As Trustee or Co-Trustee under your will, banks will manage your securities, real estate investments, other property, and business enterprises of all kinds. Specified sums of income or principal—or amounts which, in the bank's discretion, will provide adequately for your beneficiaries—will be paid as you direct. Regular reports are made to those concerned.

Guardian or Conservator:

Banks may be appointed Guardian of the estates of minors and incompetents, and Conservator of the estates of persons who are unable to care for or manage their property because of advanced age, illness, or other infirmity. Full management of securities and properties of all types is provided by the bank.

Living Trust:

You may set aside property in a Living Trust for your own benefit, for your family, or for other designated beneficiaries. You may add or withdraw capital and amend the trust at some future time. You may have the trust terminate at your death or continue for your beneficiaries. Living Trusts are completely flexible and designed to meet your particular wishes.

Life Insurance Trusts are Living Trusts under which banks are designated as the beneficiary of a customer's life insurance policies. The bank's duties are usually limited to holding the policies during the lifetime of the trustor. Under an unfunded trust, the insured himself pays the premiums. In a funded trust the insured deposits securities, the income of which is sufficient to pay the premiums. Upon the death of the insured the bank collects the proceeds, and invests them. As trustee, the bank is usually given broad powers of discretion in disbursing funds to meet the changing needs of the beneficiary.

The Composite Trust is a special form of Living Trust developed to provide flexible investment arrangements, so that the person creating the trust may—by a simple written direction—either retain full authority, direct the trustee to furnish definite investment recommendations, or direct the trustee to assume full management. The trustor designates the service best suited to his needs and circumstances at the time, and pays the charges applicable to the duties performed.

Small Trust Program—the bank's Small Trusts provide Living Trust advantages for a greater number of people. A Small Trust may be established with as little as $5,000 and includes flexible plans for family protection with participation (if qualified) in a Diversified Common Trust Fund.

Diversified Common Trust Fund:

Diversified Common Trust Fund is an investment medium for trusts under wills, guardianships, and living trusts. Flexibility in meeting the investment needs of each guardianship or trust is provided by varying the ratios of participation in each of the four separate funds: Fund "A," invested solely in common stocks; Fund "B," invested in bonds, preferred stocks, real estate loans, and other fixed income securities; Fund "C," invested in municipal bonds; Fund "D," invested in common stocks which generally stress capital appreciation more than current income.

Investment Management:

If you own securities and lack the time or the experience to manage them efficiently, you may obtain either full management or limited advisory service at a bank. In either case, your investments are under the supervision of the bank. Custody of securities is provided as part of this service.

Agency for Management of Real Estate—acting as your agent, banks can provide invaluable help in caring for your real property. They will pay taxes, insurance, maintenance costs; collect rents; and maintain full management supervision.

Custodianship of Securities:

Custodianship service provides care and attention to the details of handling securities, insuring proper attention to the collection of income and principal, the exercise of rights, actions in connection with capital adjustments, etc. A Custodian Account provides safekeeping for your securities and reports which facilitate the preparation of your income tax returns.

Escrow Service:

Whether you are buying or selling a house, vacant land, business property, or a business, you may deposit all necessary papers and funds in escrow with many banks. This service protects you by guaranteeing that all requirements are fulfilled before the transaction is completed.

Corporate Trust Services:

Banks offer many kinds of Corporate Trust Service to corporations, brokers, and government agencies. As transfer agent, registrar, dividend disbursing agent, trustee, fiscal or paying agent, corporate depository, or agent in a number of other specialized capacities involving stocks and bonds, the bank can effect many savings for customers because of its statewide facilities and trained personnel.

MUNICIPAL FINANCIAL SERVICES

Loans to Political Subdivisions:

Many municipalities find it necessary to secure funds during tax and revenue dry periods. Temporary borrowing may be in the form of tax anticipation notes, registered warrants and other forms of indebtedness as prescribed in the government code. Banks bid for, accept, discount, and carry the various types of paper at reasonable rates of interest and cooperate in other ways to assist local governments meet financial needs.

Equipment Financing—Political Subdivisions:

Municipalities can obtain equipment financing through banks for the purchase of motor vehicles and all types of other equipment.

Municipal Financial Consulting:

To meet community needs effectively, and at the same time finance at the most economical rate commensurate with market conditions, requires professional advice. Banks can analyze the problem, assess the need, and advise the steps to be taken by municipalities with financial or growth problems.

Municipal Credit Analysis:

Many banks regularly publish reports covering general obligations and revenue bond financing in every regional district, county, and community.

Purchase and Sale of Municipal Securities:

Banks bid on selected bond issues throughout the United States. Banks also deal in short-term obligations of local housing authorities and redevelopment agencies. These bonds and notes are made available to other dealers, investors, and customers of the bank. Customers can also buy and sell any tax-exempt securities through their bank.

INTERNATIONAL BANKING SERVICES

Foreign Exchange:

Through some banks you may arrange to buy or sell foreign exchange arising from incoming and out-going remittances, imports, or exports—and the settlement of foreign securities—at the most favorable rate of exchange.

Commercial Letters of Credit:

Banks issue Letters of Credit to facilitate payments under import and export transactions. Letters of Credit provide a measure of protection to both buyer and seller. They assure the client that he will be called upon to pay for his imports only if the terms and conditions of the credit have been met. They also assure him that he will obtain payment for his exports upon presentation of proper documents to the bank.

Travelers Letters of Credit:

By means of a Travelers Letter of Credit, bank customers may obtain funds at designated banks around the world, without running the risk of loss or theft of funds.

Foreign Drafts:

Drafts drawn on branches or correspondent banks abroad are available at all banks for the purpose of making payments to individuals and firms in foreign countries. Drafts may be issued in foreign currency or in U.S. dollars, depending upon exchange control regulations applicable to the country. U.S. dollar drafts, upon presentation overseas, are payable in foreign currency at drawee's buying rate for banker's checks on New York or San Francisco.

Collections and Discounts:

Bank customers are assured prompt handling of all collection items drawn against drawees outside the United States. In addition, exporters often find it advantageous to obtain financing by means of advances against their documentary collections.

Foreign Credit Information:

Banks can promptly provide accurate credit information on practically all major foreign banks and commercial houses. Credit data on other concerns, and on individuals, can also be obtained readily—anywhere in the world—through appropriate sources abroad.

Foreign Trade Services:

Through its Foreign Trade Services Section, a bank can help clients find new foreign outlets for their products and develop new sources of supply abroad. The bank can also assist in establishing working relationships—such as joint ventures, distributorships, and representatives—in foreign countries.

APPENDIX II

Selected List of Readings in Banking

Banks and Banking

Annual Report of the Board of Governors of the Federal Reserve System Covering Operations of the Year. Annual.

Annual Report of the Comptroller of the Currency. U.S. Treasury Dept. Annual.

Annual Report of the Federal Deposit Insurance Corporation. Annual.

Annual Report of—State Superintendent of Banks.

Assets, Liabilities, and Capital Accounts, Commercial and Mutual Savings Banks. Federal Deposit Insurance Corporation. Semiannual. Statistics by types of banks and by states.

Bank Management (3rd ed.), Walter Kennedy. Bankers Publishing Company, 1963. $9.75. Directed to the medium-sized bank and written primarily for bank executives. It includes recent banking developments.

Bank Terminology. National Cash Register Company, 1962.

Banking and Monetary Statistics. Board of Governors of the Federal Reserve System, 1943. Out of print. Supplements as they become available are announced in the *Federal Reserve Bulletin.*

The Economics of Money and Banking (3rd ed.), Harper,

1959. "This book . . . employs theoretical, institutional, and historical approaches."

Federal Reserve Act of 1913 with Amendments and Laws Relating to Banking. U.S. Laws, Statutes, etc., 1958. Distributed by U.S. Government Printing Office.

The Library of Money and Credit. Prentice-Hall, 1962–1964, 18 vols. $87.72. Prepared for the Commission on Money and Credit by outstanding authorities and financial institutions. Individual volumes may be purchased separately.

The Practical Operation and Management of a Bank. Marshall C. Corns. Bankers Publishing Co., 1962. 2 vols. Covers virtually every phase of banking. Good as introduction to the field of commercial banking.

Bibliographies, General

Canadian Government Publications. Canada, Department of Public Printing and Stationery. Monthly.

Current Publications, Bureau of Statistics (Canada) 1960, with supplements.

Government Publications. Her Majesty's Stationery Office. Monthly.

Guide to U.S. Government Statistics; 3rd ed. by John L. Andriot. Documents Index, 1961. An annotated guide to publications by departments and agencies, with detailed subject index.

Marketing Information Guide. U.S. Department of Commerce. Monthly. Distributed by U.S. Government Printing Office. A comprehensive annotated guide to current marketing and related publications.

Monthly Catalog of United States Government Publications. U.S. Government Printing Office. Monthly.

Dictionaries

Dictionary of Business and Finance, Donald T. Clark and Bert A. Gottfreid. Crowell, 1957. Arranged by both master and specific entries and based on contemporary usage.

Directories

Directory of Business and Financial Services, ed. by Mary A. McNierney. Special Libraries Association, 1963.

Industrial Directories. American Marketing Association, 1963. An annotated, descriptive list of state industrial directories, with full bibliographic information on how to obtain them.

Polk's Bank Directory. R. L. Polk and Company. Semi-annual with supplements.

Poor's Register of Corporations, Directors, and Executives, United States and Canada. Standard and Poor's Corporation. Annual with three supplements. Includes individual data of directors and executives in separate alphabet.

Rand McNally International Bankers Directory. Semi-annual with supplements.

Encyclopedias

Encyclopedia of Banking and Finance (Glenn G. Munn); 7th ed. by F. L. Garcia. Bankers Publishing Company, 1973. A comprehensive exposition of the financial system and terms included therein.

Indexes

Business Periodicals Index. H. W. Wilson Company. Monthly, with cumulations.

Canadian Index to Periodicals and Documentary Films. Canadian Library Association. Monthly, annually, and quinquennially.

Funk and Scott Index of Corporations and Industries. Investment Index Company. Weekly. Indexes some 200 periodicals and services featuring financial, industrial, and corporate news.

Periodicals

American Banker. Daily.

Bank and Quotation Record. William B. Dana Company. Monthly. A companion publication to the *Commercial and Financial Chronicle.*

Bank of England Quarterly Bulletin. Quarterly.

Bank of Montreal Business Review. Monthly.

Bank of Nova Scotia Monthly Review. Monthly.

The Banker (London). Monthly.

Bankers Magazine. Bankers' Publishing Co. Quarterly.

Bankers Monthly. Rand McNally. Monthly.

Banking. The American Bankers Association. Monthly.

Barron's. Dow-Jones and Company. Weekly.

Business Cycle Developments. U.S. Dept of Commerce. Monthly. Distributed by U.S. Government Printing Office. Brings together many available economic indicators. Data is speedily gathered for the business cycle studies.

Business Week. McGraw-Hill. Weekly.

Canadian Banker. Canadian Banker's Association. Quarterly.

Canadian Statistical Review. Canada. Bureau of Statistics. Monthly; with weekly supplements. Distributed by Queen's Printer.

Commercial and Financial Chronicle. William B. Dana Company. Semiweekly. Monday (complete statistical issue, market quotation records, corporation news, bank clearings, state and city news, etc.); Thursday (general news, interpretative articles, and advertising).

Economic Indicators. U.S. Congress, Joint Economic Committee. Monthly. Distributed by U.S. Government Printing Office. Prepared by the Council of Economic Advisers.

Economist (London). Weekly.

Federal Reserve Bulletin. Board of Governors of the Federal Reserve System. Monthly. June and December issues list separate releases available. Each District Federal Reserve bank publishes a *Monthly Review* for its area, also available.

Finance. Finance Publishing Corporation. Monthly.

International Financial Statistics. International Monetary Fund. Monthly.

Monetary Indicators. Mellon National Bank and Trust Company. Weekly. Apply. Graphs and comment; and a continuous series of indicators.

Money, Interest Rates, and Government Securities. Goldsmith-Nagan Washington Service. Biweekly. A financial newsletter useful to bank bond departments.

Monthly Digest of Statistics. U.K. Central Statistical Office. Monthly. Distributed by Her Majesty's Stationery Office.

Monthly Economic Letter. First National City Bank of New York. Monthly.

Monthly Labor Review. U.S. Department of Labor. Monthly. Distributed by U.S. Government Printing Office.

National Banking Reviews. Comptroller of the Currency, U.S. Treasury Dept. Quarterly. Subtitle: A journal of policy and practice.

New York Times. Daily and Sunday.

Reporting on Governments, by Sylvia Porter. Weekly. Subtitle: Weekly analysis and forecast on U.S. Government securities, Washington monetary policies, and trends in interest rates.

Statistical Bulletin. U.S. Securities and Exchange Commission. Monthly. Covering the securities exchanges, new securities offerings, and registrations.

Statistical Indicator. Statistical Indicator Associates. Weekly. A compilation of extensive economic indicators, with comment.

Survey of Current Business. U.S. Department of Commerce. Monthly, with weekly supplements. Supplements as issued. Distributed by U.S. Government Printing Office.

Trust and Estates. Fiduciary Publishers, Inc. Monthly.

United States Government Securities. Mellon National Bank and Trust Company. Quarterly. Apply. Descriptive data on Government securities; discontinued savings bonds; values and yields; interest tables.

Wall Street Journal. Daily. Published in Eastern, Midwest, Pacific Coast, and Southwest editions.

Washington Banktrends. Washington News Features. Weekly. Rates on request. A weekly appraisal of economic, financial, political developments.

Additional Selected Readings

The Bankers by Martin Mayer, 1974, Weybright and Talley.

Money and Banking Analysis and Policy by Charles R. Whittlesey, Arthur M. Freeman and Edward S. Herman, 1968, 2nd Edition, Macmillan Company.

Money and Banking by Raymond P. Kent, 1972, 6th Edition, Holt, Rinehart and Winston, Inc.

Money and Banking by Eugene S. Klise, 1972, 5th Edition, South-Western Publishing Company.

Money and Banking by Charles L. Prather, 1969, 9th Edition, Richard D. Irwin, Inc.

Money and Banking and Public Policy by Harold Barger, 1968, 2nd Edition, Rand McNally & Company.

Money, Banking and the United States Economy, by Harry D. Hutchinson, 1971, 2nd Edition, Appleton-Century Crofts.

The Money Men of Europe by Paul Ferris, 1968, The Macmillan Company.

The One-Bank Holding Company, A Group of Essays, edited by Herbert V. Prochnow, 1969, Rand McNally & Co.

Readings in Money and Banking, Edited by Harold A. Wolf and R. Conrad Doenges, 1968, Appleton-Century-Crofts.

The Swiss Banks by T. R. Fehrenbach, 1966, McGraw-Hill Book Company.